AMERICAN CITIZEN

I feel it is quite appropriate that the actual stone litho label that is a part of this book would bear this title. Cigar labels and the cigar industry dominated the American scene for almost three quarters of a century and will always be an important part of our American History. Although hundreds of themes were experimented with to market cigars, American pride and patriotism were uppermost in the minds of our Fathers and Grandfathers who lived in this Golden Era. Created at the turn of the century when hard work and pride in craftsmanship were still held in high esteem, this original label gives us a brief but lasting glimpse at that era.

THE ART OF THE
CIGAR
LABEL
JOE DAVIDSON

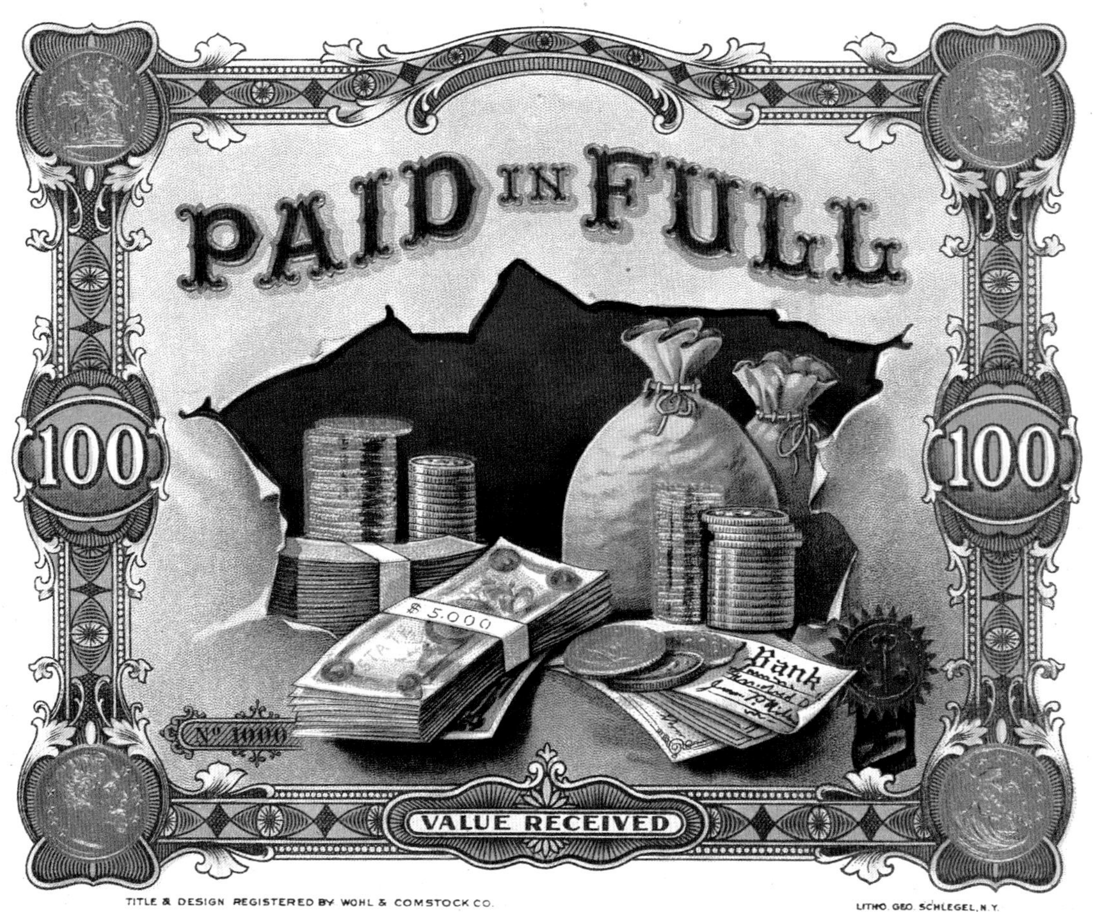
PAID IN FULL
100
100
VALUE RECEIVED
TITLE & DESIGN REGISTERED BY WOHL & COMSTOCK CO.
LITHO. GEO. SCHLEGEL, N.Y.

PAID IN FULL

WELLFLEET

110 Enterprise Avenue
Secaucus, NJ 07094

Publishing Director: Frank Oppel
Editorial Director: Tony Meisel
Design Director: Carmela Pereira
Editor: Theresa Koziol
Composition: Meadowcomp Ltd..
Origination and Printing: Palace Press

Manufactured in Singapore.
ISBN: 1-55521-436-3

Contents

INTRODUCTION

As more and more items of memorabilia enter the expanding world of collectibles, it can never be said that cigar labels took the collectibles market by storm when they first started emerging from dusty old warehouses and abandoned factories back in the 1960's. They were a bit of an enigma for the flea market and antique dealers who first discovered them, because although they were extremely beautiful to look at, they were too "new looking" for their level of customer, plus, there was not an already established core of collectors out there ready and waiting as in other ephemera markets such as postcards and posters.

For almost a decade, these outstandingly beautiful examples of chromolithographic art which cost up to $6,000 per design to launch during the turn of the century, lay dormant on flea market tables with neither buyers or sellers truly understanding their importance or value. They could very well be sitting on those same tables right now except for a combination of events that took place in the late 1970's.

Taking a quantum leap over the flea market level and every progressive retail level above them, beautifully framed cigar labels appeared in three Bloomingdale's department stores during the 1978 Christmas season and were selling "briskly" at $79.95 each! At the very same time, major Fortune 500 companies like 3M Company in St. Paul, Minnesota and Mead Paper Company in Dayton, Ohio gave hundreds of them away as "executive gifts" to their most important clients. On September 7, 1979, *The Wall Street Journal* published a feature story on their front page about the explosive growth in popularity of cigar labels as both collectibles and investments.

Old time dealers who had seen thousands of cigar labels pass through their hands for pennies attempted to dismiss this new popularity as a short term fad or fluke, but the die was now cast, and after being marketed successful by some of the most prestigious retailers in the country, cigar labels graduated to their rightful place in the world of art. In an attempt to explain how cigar labels gained their status as the high water mark of the advertising illustrators art, the following chapters will give you a brief history of the growth of both the tobacco industry and the lithography industry and their unique relationship which helped both of them grow dramatically.

I have also tried to give you as many insights as possible into values, collecting, identifying old labels and the innovative ways that lithographers and cigar makers attempted to attract the eyes and nickels of our forefathers. I am sure you will appreciate the fact that this book is not an effort to memorialize the Joe Davidson collection, but to give you an overview of the broad range of themes that are available to you as a collector.

With thousands of subjects to choose from, I made a concerted effort to feature a large number of labels that are available on the open market. A testimonial to that effort is the fact that over 90% of the labels pictured herein are available to you. Undoubtedly, your appreciation of cigar label art will be heightened by understanding all the processes by which they came into being and their placement in history, and I hope I have covered all of those bases for you. I do apologize in advance if your favorite image does not appear within, but I am sure that you will understand most of my choices when you consider the restrictions of space vs. the thousands of images available. On the brighter side, it's possible your favorite is a super rare label worth over $1,000!

If you still have any unanswered questions concerning cigar art or chromolithography in general, I am pleased to be part of a recently formed organization called The *American Antique Graphics Society* to whom you can write any inquiries.

The American Antique Graphics Society
P. O. Box 924
Medina, Ohio 44256

ACKNOWLEDGEMENTS

Despite the fact that I, like most authors like to think of their works as a one man effort, there have been hundreds of individuals over the last decade who have contributed in a variety of ways to make this book possible. Quite a few people stand out, and I apologize to any that I may have omitted.

I owe special and recent debt to John Grossman, the world reknown design artist and president of the "Gifted Line" who has contributed a number of labels from the Grossman collection to appear in this book.

John has attempted (and quite successfully) to keep alive the outstanding images used on cigar labels during the Golden Era by tastefully reproducing them on high quality gift wrap, playing cards, ashtrays, mugs, and a score of other products from examples held in his massive collection of cigar label art.

Acknowledgements too must be given Bernhard and Bina von Schubert, present owners of the famous 420 year old, Klingenberg Litho in Germany. Their efforts to keep alive the lost art of Stone Lithography and their maintenance and curation of their spectacular archive of cigar labels, posters and stones has my greatest admiration. These extremely dedicated art lovers gave me unlimited access to their historical records, photo archive and label books to help me in providing examples in this book for you.

It has also been my good fortune to work with Dr. Tony Hyman, author of a number of books and articles relating to the cigar industry.

As an author, educator and historian, Tony has dedicated a major portion of his life to researching the history of the cigar industry, and more recently, all types of collectibles, to help educate the general public as to the treasures they may own.

In spite of his hectic schedule of TV appearances and lectures, Tony has always found time to get back to me with answers to perplexing questions.

He also has amassed a spectacular collection of rare and valuable cigar boxes over the last three decades which would be the envy of any collector.

Many thanks also go to Dr. Glen Westfall, History Professor at the University of South Florida at Tampa, who did his doctoral dissertation on Vincente Ybor and has written many books and articles on the history of Tampa and the cigar industry.

The efforts that this man has put forth in acquiring important collections for his university and for the Tampa Historical Society could not be matched anywhere. He is also responsible for tracking down the von Schubert family in Germany for me for which I will be ever thankful.

Another prominent historian who needs special recognition is Thomas Vance, great-grandson of Ignacio Haya, founder of the Sanchez & Haya Factory #1 in Tampa.

Although Mr. Vance is an expert in a variety of collectibles, his first love has always been cigar label art, and owns one of the more outstanding collections in the world.

Because of his lifetime experiences as a Tampa and cigar industry historian, Mr. Vance is called upon quite frequently by museums and universities for his knowledge and appraisals. Many of the Tampa related labels in this book have been provided by Mr. Vance.

It would be impossible to acknowledge all the helpful librarians and museum curators across this country who have assisted me in digging through tons of musty old directories and records, but I must single out Jennifer Williams from the Education Department of the Detroit Institute of Art who spent over a year compiling information and data on the heretofore unrecognized Calvert Litho and sharing all her discoveries with me.

Other institutions that contributed include the American Tobacco Museum, The Smithsonian Institute, The Western Reserve Historical Society, The Library of Congress, The Windsor Art Museum in Canada, The Museum Of American Folk Art, and the University of South Florida.

Individual art lovers, collectors and historians who were of great assistance through the years include George Schlegel III, Lois Tomasky, Charlotte Edwards, Joseph J. Hruby, Ed Kilcline, Thomas Somerville, Richard Revolinski, David and Larry Lisot, David Masten, Leif Erickson, Don Pickett, Mark Trout, Bruce Ferrini, Louis Van Duren, Mike Stinnett, Jerry Senion, David Elk, Blaine and Annabelle Stewart, Billie D. Tarpley, Leonard L. Lasko, Valerie Olander, Teri Flaherty, Mary Kreitzer, Arthur Fuente, Betty Wetzel, Hank Hatch, Charles H. Klein, Polly Mays, Avi Greenbaum, Curt Bogen and hard working photographer Mary Russell. And most of all to my wife Sue and my son Aaron, who helped more than I could ever express.

TOBACCO

Tobacco is a dirty weed–I like it.
It satisfies no normal need–I like it.
It makes you thin, it makes you lean,
It takes the hair right off your bean,
It's the worst darn stuff I've ever seen–I like it.
–"Tobacco" by Graham Lee Hemminger

omano Pano, a Spanish monk who accompanied Christopher Columbus on his second trip to America, first wrote about tobacco in his book *Indian Rituals.* He speaks of a plant called "cohabba" or "guioja" by the natives. The leaves were smoked in forked pipes called "tabacco" or "tobacco". The Spanish called tobacco *yerba sancta* or holy herb, so we must conclude the name we use comes from the pipe rather than the plant.

Another of Columbus' crew members, Rodrigo de Jerez, was probably one of the first people to be persecuted for smoking. He was arrested while strolling down the street with this strange firebrand in his mouth and blowing smoke out of his nose. The mentality of the Spanish Inquisition reasoned that anyone who blew smoke out of his nose must be in league with the devil, so he was given seven years in prison!

The first to describe tobacco as a medicinal herb was Dr. Nicolas Mernardes who wrote about the *Herbs of West Indies* published in 1574. In it, he says that Indians used tobacco as a first-rate cure for wounds. Moistened, the leaves were placed on the skull for headaches, and they were chewed as a remedy for toothaches.

In 1648, a Dutch physician wrote that tobacco was used as an antidote against wounds from poison arrows, saying that he saw with his own eyes how it rapidly cured badly infected wounds. He also said that it showed great promise for curing colic, scabies, tumors, pimples and worms. Besides using tobacco for pharmacological purposes, the Indians used it in many rituals, from placating spirits to increasing potency, and it was considered by all tribes as a gift from the heavens.

Tobacco certainly got off to a rocky start in Europe. King James I, for instance, passed laws establishing mutilation as punishment for taking a pinch of snuff, and hanging on the gibbet was the

penalty for smoking a pipe. But nothing could stop tobacco's rise in popularity. Gradually it became more plentiful and less expensive. Opposition to its use waned, and the laws were dropped from the books.

As tobacco grew in popularity in Europe, the inevitable happened: starting with James I of England, governments began to tax it. In spite of this, by the beginning of the 18th Century average consumption in Britain was about two pounds per person, with women and children counted as the heaviest smokers. It was not long before people all over the world sampled tobacco, acquired a taste for the new luxury, and wished for more at a reasonable price.

As popular as tobacco was in the United States, use was limited to snuff, pipes, and plugs until the Civil War. After the war, with industry expanding, the completion of the transcontinental railroad, and hoards of immigrants pouring into the country, times were good and people wanted to appear more refined. Undoubtedly, smoking a cigar was much more in keeping with that desire than constantly spitting and drooling tobacco juice, or snorting snuff.

When the government cut cigar taxes drastically, it put cigars within the price range of the average American. Annual consumption reached the 1 billion mark by 1870, among a population of only 40 million. By 1906, sales reached 7 billion and hit an all-time high of 8.2 billion in 1920. Incidentally, that was the year in which use of cigarettes surpassed that of cigars, and they have never given up the lead.

A woman is just a woman,
But a good cigar is a smoke.
–Rudyard Kipling

THE CIGAR INDUSTRY

Most publications and articles relating to the cigar industry that I have read over the past decade seem to dwell and concentrate on the giants of the industry, with their mergers, takeovers, battles with the unions, and the government's anti-trust suits in 1911 that broke up the tobacco monopolies. Somewhat interesting reading if you are a big business historian, but by changing a few names and dates, they all sound like a carbon copy of what's going on in today's business world.

By overlooking the small Mom & Pop cigar makers, these historians missed one of the most historical episodes in the history of our country and, of the business world. Never before and never since has an event of such magnitude taken place in history. Here was an industry, where even the lowliest immigrant, for a few dollars could buy a cutting board and a knife, a few "hands" of tobacco, some boxes and labels and be in business for himself! This was the personification of the American Dream!

By 1905, there were 70,000 Mom & Pop cigar factories registered with the Federal Government, and it is estimated that there were at least another 30,000 who never bothered to register. Here were 100,000 entrepreneurs in the United States at the Turn of the Century in just one industry!

One of the earliest pioneers was a German immigrant named Herrmann Fendrich who came to the United States with his family from Baden Baden, Germany in 1833. Herrmann was the oldest of five brothers and decided they should start a cut plug company in their new home in Baltimore. Although plug tobacco was far more popular at the time, they did start making cigars as a sideline, and their first cigar brand was called "Five Brothers" picturing the five brothers on the label.

In 1845 the family moved to New Orleans and while living there sold cigars out of the back of a wagon. This type of personal contact with the customer brought an early and lasting success for the

1. *Typical Mom & Pop cigar factory in eastern Pennsylvania, courtesy of Tony Hyman.*

2. *A typical large Florida factory, courtesy of Glen Westfall.*

Fendrich Brothers. By 1855, the brothers made their last move to Evansville, Indiana and opened a new factory and retail store. In 1877, they offered a variety of brands like *Diamond Joe, The Globe Democrat* (a St. Louis newspaper) *Red Ruby, Casa Nova, Lady Carmen, El Cuto* and others.

In 1899, after Herrmann's death, young John Fendrich took over the company. John had graduated from Notre Dame with a degree in agriculture; with this and his vast knowledge of the tobacco industry, the Fendrich Company grew to employ over 40 cigar rollers, many of them women, who were neater, cleaner and didn't smoke cigars. By the 1920's they had built a five story factory employing over 1,000 workers, but by 1966, with lagging sales, the surviving Fendrichs sold out to the Parodi Cigar Company of Scranton, Pa.

While the Fendrichs' were building their American Dream up north, a young Cuban named Vincente Ybor started his own factory in Havana, Cuba, producing the famous *El Principe de Gales* brand (Prince of Wales) registered in 1853. Ybor had to flee Havana after the outbreak of the Ten Years War (1868) and started a factory in Key West, Florida. In 1876, he expanded his operations to New York opening the "El Coloso" factory.

After a devastating fire in Key West destroyed many buildings including Ybor's factory, he decided to leave South Florida and transfer all his operations to a site on the outskirts of Tampa, which eventually became Ybor City. Don Vincente decided to build a "company town" modeled after George Pullman's successful operation in Illinois. The development would include his factory, homes for the workers and some commercial buildings. This isolated format allowed Ybor to more easily control the lives of the workers, and the labor unions would have fewer grievances.

Ignacio Haya, a close friend and advisor to Ybor purchased ten acres adjacent to Ybor's land and constructed a factory and several worker's homes. It was planned that both factories would open the same day in March, 1866, but temporary labor problems prevented Ybor from opening his *Principe de Gales* factory, and the very first cigars produced in Ybor City were produced by the Flor de Sanchez & Haya factory.

The rapid growth of Ybor City attests to the success of these Latin cigar manufacturers to import large numbers of immigrants to work in their factories. Census records show that Tampa had 720 residents in 1880, and by 1890 it had grown to 5,532, mostly Latins. Ybor City was a wild "frontier town" with no law and order until June 2, 1887 when it was annexed into the city of Tampa. Al-

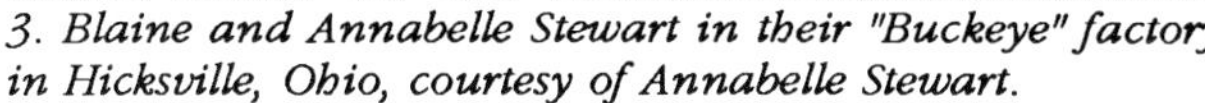
3. Blaine and Annabelle Stewart in their "Buckeye" factory in Hicksville, Ohio, courtesy of Annabelle Stewart.

CUESTA, REY $ CO.'S FACTORY, TAMPA, FLORIDA.

4. Exterior of the old Cuesta-Rey Factory in Tampa, Florida, courtesy of Glen Westfall.

though Ybor fought the annexation, one of the main benefits was the appearance of Tampa policemen patrolling the streets which made it a much safer place to visit.

One of the most unique pieces of culture the Cuban immigrant cigar workers brought with them to the United States was the innovation of the "lector" or reader. Every morning the reader would arrive at the factory with his co-workers and get into his small pulpit overlooking the work area or wander among the work tables. He would usually begin by reading the local Spanish newspaper at the top of his voice from cover to cover. In the afternoons, he would sometimes read Spanish classic novels or ballads. Most of the people working in these cigar factories were completely uneducated, but felt a great need to improve their culture and stay on top of current events. Interestingly enough, the readers were not employed by the cigar company, but by the *workers* themselves! Each cigar worker paid 25¢ per week for his services, and it was not uncommon to find a cigar reader making $125.00 a week!

For a change of pace, some of the employees of the larger cigar factories employed a piano player in the afternoons, but the readers were by far the most popular and became extremely influential with both the owners and workers. Today, Tampa's surviving cigar factories don't employ lectors anymore, in fact, with the advent of mechanization and mass production, the hand roller is becoming more of a dinosaur in this country except for a few special brands.

On a recent tour of the Cuesta-Rey Factory in Tampa, I was surprised to see the tremendous volume they were capable of producing with a minimum of employees. There is still a considerable amount of hand work by some employees with the large wrapper leaves, but the fast moving machines do all the rest at lightning speed.

Interestingly enough, this extremely successful company owned by the Newman Family has its cigar making roots in Cleveland, Ohio. The original company was started by the grandfather, J. C. Newman, who came to the U.S. from Austria in 1889 at the age of 14. The family settled in Cleve-

A once-familiar scene in Florida's cigar factories—
the hired reader entertaining cigar rollers

5. A "Lector" reading to cigar rollers in Florida, courtesy of Glen Westfall.

6. Interior scene of old cigar store, courtesy of Tony Hyman.

land, Ohio and at the age of 17, after learning the ins and outs of the cigar business as an immigrant roller, he started his own small business, rolling cigars during the day and selling them in the evening to wholesale grocers.

By 1895 he was able to rent a store and hire five rollers. In 1899, he hired his first salesman and business began to boom. By 1903, at age 28, Newman had the largest cigar factory of over 100 registered in Cleveland, producing Cleveland's leading brand, *Judge Wright* which survived for many decades. *Student Prince* and *Rigoletto* were two more of their brands you may be familiar with. In 1954, the family moved their operations to Tampa, Florida in an effort to keep alive their cigar making tradition.

Another famous cigar making family, but on a much smaller scale were the founders of the Blaine Stewart Cigar Company of Hicksville, Ohio, Blaine and Annabelle Stewart. Blaine and Annabelle were outstanding examples of American entrepreneurism by successfully competing with the larger mechanized factories and continued to hand-roll cigars in their small factory up until 1981 when they retired at the ages of 77 and 78.

The Ohio Senate adopted a resolution, #807, on January 21, 1982 honoring the Stewarts for their lifelong dedication to quality and hard work and as the owners of the last hand-rolled cigar factory in Ohio. Blaine has since passed on, but Annabelle is alive and well and could probably still roll 1,000 cigars a day as she did in the past. Their beautifully cared for homestead with the tiny 20 x 20 foot "factory" in the back which looked like a summer cottage has been sold off, but whenever I see a *Double Elk, Elkmont, Spinning Maid, Bachelor Girl,* or *Sophomore* cigar label, I will always remember this beautiful couple.

STONE LITHOGRAPHY

[Greek, Lithos-a stone/ Grapho-write]
Stone Lithography/Chromolithography/Photomechanical Printing

n the hope of giving a helping hand to those who are interested in building a collection of high quality artworks, whether they were created for the cigar industry or any other purpose, I will try to give you enough facts to let you distinguish stone lithography from photomechanical printing, and to recognize the in-between stages. It is certainly impossible to cover in one chaper all of the graphic processes used. In any case, many of the intaglio, relief, and planographic processes were seldom used for cigar art.

The art of stone lithography was born out of poverty and necessity, when Aloys Senefelder of Prague, Bohemia, at the age of 23 found himself forced to provide for a family of nine. A playwright, Senefelder was also a "true" inventor, never cowed by negativism, always hopeful, ingenious and tireless. When he found it too expensive to get his plays published, he decided to find an inexpensive way to become his own publisher and printer.

His first breakthrough came in 1796 when he found that the local Bavarian Limestone made an excellent printing surface for a crude relief process. It was soft enough to be grooved with a tool to make a raised image for printing, yet hard enough for repeated impressions.

In 1798, he gave to the world a third printing process, neither relief, as from type, not intaglio, as from etching. It was a flat surface (planographic) method that opened whole new horizons. Senefelder discovered that if the image is drawn directly on the flat surface of the stone with a waxy crayon, the porous stone allows the grease from the crayon to penetrate and become fixed in the stone. The stone, now ready to print on, is dampened with water, the moisture being repelled by the areas containing the grease, but absorbed into the other areas. When an ink roller is passed over the surface, no ink is taken up by the damp areas, but the lines and dots of the grease drawings attract the ink, and hold it until transferring the clear image to the paper passing through the press. Senefelder called his process "chemical printing;" we know it as Stone Lithography. It proved to be a fast, inexpensive method that produced a true image, with all of the tonal effects that rival the velvety qualities of Mezzotints. Although this description deals with single-color lithographs, practically all of it is applicable in describing the process of multi-colored printing, or "Chromolithographs."

In 1808 Senefelder published a book with illustrations by Albrecht Durër. The quality of the illustrations revealed the possibilities of stone lithography as an art medium as well as for commercial printing. Lithography is truly art for the artist. The artist is totally involved from beginning to end, from preparing the stone, drawing the image, selecting the colors to supervising the printing.

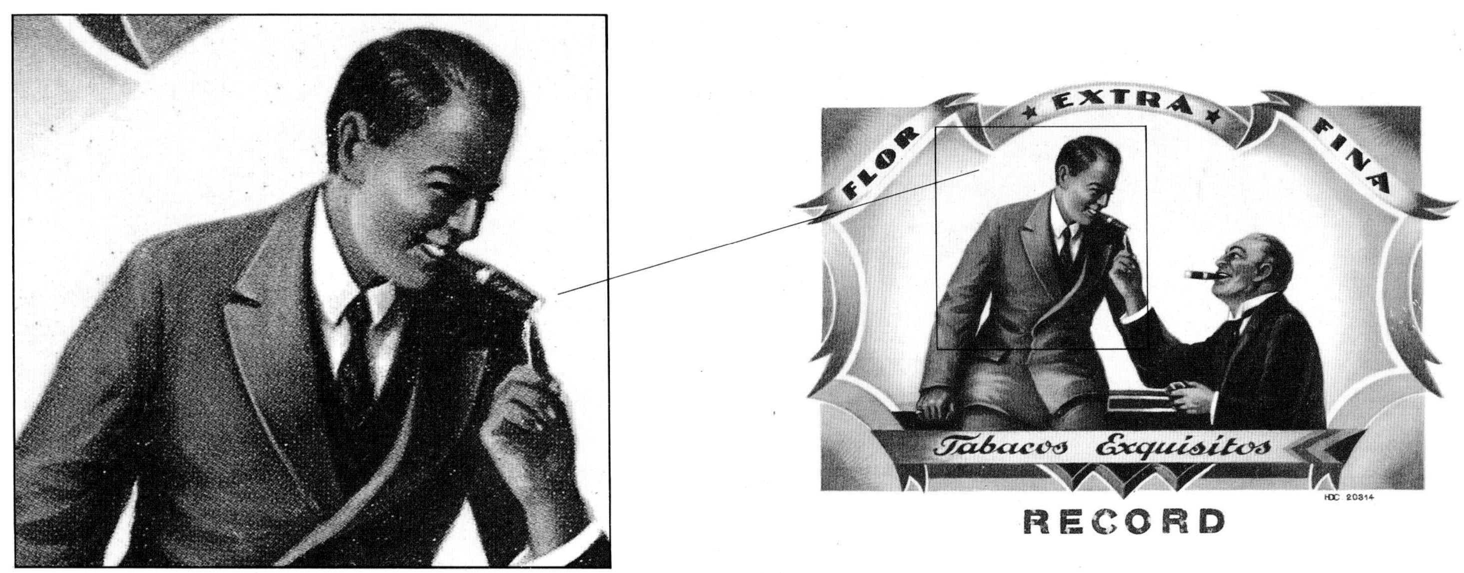

Photomechanical

Frederick Goulding, famous printer of both etchings and lithographs put it well, saying, "Lithography is not a reproduction; it is a replica, a multiplication of copies; not a facsimile or a paraphrase, but the actual drawing. That is where it differs from so many other processes."

Benjamin West, an American artist working in England, created one of the first works of true artistic merit on stone, "An Angel at the Tomb of Christ," which received worldwide acclaim.

But it was in France, starting around 1809, that lithography found its heart and soul, blossoming under such reknowned artists as Honoré Daumier, Theodore Gericault, Eugene Delacroix and Spanish artist Francisco Goya, whose lithographs command top dollar today.

In 1836, also in France, Godefroi Engelmann and his son, Jean, invented a method of color printing which came to be called Chromolithography. Using red, yellow and blue pigments, the Engelmanns and painter William Wyld together produced a seven stone color image from crayon and lithographic inks. This was indeed a major step forward in only one generation since Senefelder's first efforts, and a giant advance beyond the hand-colored lithographs.

Stone Lithography in the United States reached its pinnacle with the work of Louis Prang, who came to Boston from Germany. Prang developed methods using up to 25 stones to achieve unusual

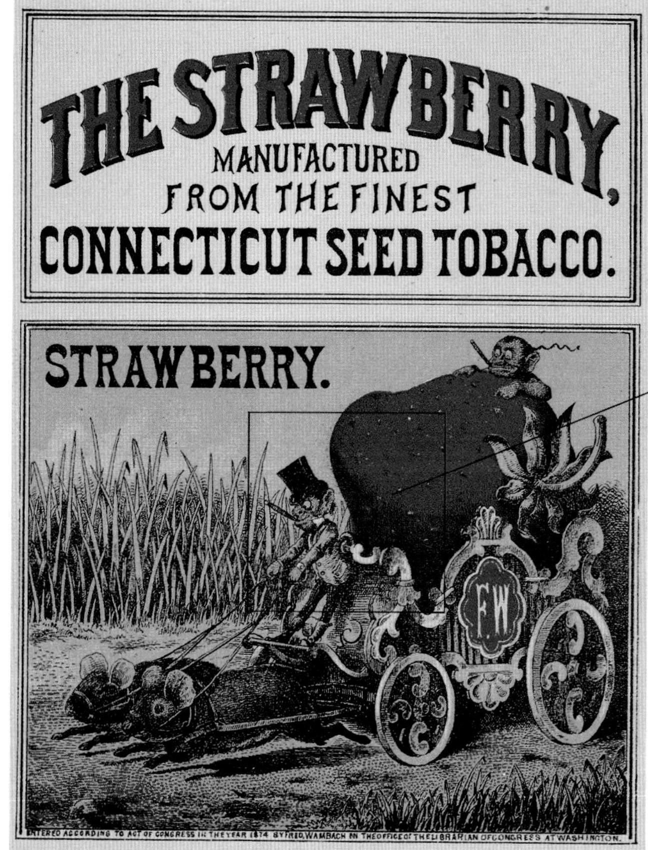

Crayon Method

color layering and added an embossing process for the creation of imitation brush strokes, plus a superb lacquering process of the finished product. Given the title of Father of Chromolithography in the United States, Prang was responsible also for the introduction of the first American greeting cards in 1837.

The earliest chromolithographs were made up of solid blocks of colors placed side by side. What Prang had developed was a technique to produce the entire color spectrum by intermingling small color areas, which, after all the 12 (or 20 if necessary) runs had been made, created the complete range of hues and tints for a realistic looking final image.

By the turn of the century, the process had become even more sophisticated by the use of hand stippling. In simple terms, stippling is the use of a series of intermingled dots that produce varient degrees of shading. This process had been used in engravings as far back as the 16th Century, and was brought into prominence by the artist Bartolozzi in the latter 18th century. Using this concept with color allowed the printer to produce an extremely accurate rendition of the artist's original painting. As lithographers worked diligently to continually upgrade the quality of their product, there was also a need to speed up production in an effort to meet the demand for more and more high quality advertising artworks.

The litho stones were extremely heavy and hard to handle, many of them weighing as much as 600 pounds, and they also broke easily. When it was found that zinc or aluminum surfaces could be prepared so that they produced prints with all the characteristics of those from stones, thin plates of those metals were substituted for the heavy stones. To adapt the method to the rotary printing press, a thinner version of the metal plates were used, to curve and attach to a cylindrical roller,

Stipple Method

allowing for more speed and efficiency. This method, along with the stones that were still used by many printers, made up the lion's share of the color printing market until the late 1920's, when the photomechanical process gained in popularity.

The latter process, which is still in use today, is a technique whereby the original artwork is photographed through a set of color filters, breaking the picture into four separate colors: yellow, red, blue and black. This produces a half-tone plate consisting of an array of closely spaced dots, which is placed in front of the photographic plate. The plate is rotated to varying angles for each of the four colors, so that the four sets of dots interface with one another as little as possible. When the four plates are printed, each color appears in its own assigned area, in some cases falling over each other to modify, make other colors, or, sometimes obliterate each other. The dots can be made so marvelously fine that there can be up to 400 dots per linear inch. For ordinary printing purposes, a screen having 120 dots to an inch is generally used; coarser newspaper photos use 60 dots per inch.

Sadly, the new four-color process eliminated the need for the lithographic artist. Plates could now be produced straight from the original art to the photomechanical process. Of course, this greatly reduced the cost of label production, but it also brought to an end to the era that brought us some of the finest examples of Chromolithography ever produced. As the late 1920's saw the decline of cigar smoking, so also it began the decline of the quality of cigar label art.

To help you identify the methods of printing I have discussed, here are examples of the crayon method of chromolithography, the stipple method, and the photomechanical process. Armed with a magnifying glass, you will be able to quickly identify what you are considering buying, and protect yourself from purchasing a worthless photomechanical reproduction. This applies not only to cigar label art, but to any color graphics you may be examining.

EMBOSSING & GILDING

y the early 1890's the lithographers introduced another step in the manufacturing of cigar labels in an effort to give them a three dimensional effect. Brass embossing dies were engraved to coincide with the image on the label. A raised "male" die and a depressed "female" die which, when aligned with the image in a thirty-ton press permanently embossed the label, giving it three dimensional qualities.

Another process, introduced and coordinated with embossing was "gilding" which either utilized genuine gold leaf, (used primarily by German and Cuban printers) or "bronzing" in which bronze powder was mixed with lacquer or sizing, applied like ink, then burnished with brushes or

Embossing Machine

Bronzing Machine

polished rollers to make them gleam like gold.

Much rarer than the gold leafed or bronzed labels are those that appear to have silver on the coins, medals or trim. In all the different labels I perused over the last 20 years, I can honestly only recall about a dozen.

I brought this point up while interviewing George Schlegel III who told me that experiments using silver and aluminum powders similar to the bronzing method created a number of hazards and at least two deaths were caused from minor explosions while working with these products.

Since the gold and bronzing methods proved much safer and easier to work with, and created an extremely attractive finished product, attempts at adding the silver "look" were dropped causing those surviving examples to become extremely rare and coveted. Although gilding increased production costs, the dramatic results more than justified the slight increase.

When people talk about the "Golden Era" of cigar labels, many collectors associate that with the introduction of gilding and embossing in the 1890's up to the late 1920's when the less attractive photomechanical labels began to appear.

LITHOGRAPHERS & LABEL BROKERS

An entire book could be written about lithographers and label brokers alone. But since our concern is with the relationship between lithographers and the cigar industry, I will content myself with showing the highlights of the major cigar labels producers and how they grew, telling of some of the mergers and acquisitions, and providing you with a list of those who marketed cigar labels. I hope this will help in your identification of the names appearing on your labels and artworks.

As an educator, I have always stressed the importance of research. In this regard, it's been my good fortune to have had access to important documents, publications and biographies from which I've been able to glean many interesting and little known facts that made the cigar era totally unique. It was a particular blessing to have had the privilege of sitting down with and interviewing a number of the people who actually worked and grew up in the business. Among these individuals, in their 70's and 80's, the most notable was George Schlegel III.

By the time George was born, Schlegel Litho was already a major producer of beautiful 12- to 22-color chromolithographs to a variety of industries, including the cigar business. George grew up in New York society, attended Princeton and the Naval Academy, and became involved in the family business at the age of 21, becoming president when he was 39.

I discovered George in 1980, and have leaned heavily on him through the years for answers to the questions that never were addressed in the tons of publications I pored through in library basements. He had a knack for getting straight to the answer, clearly and logically instead of getting bogged down in technocratic theories. A prime example of this came when I asked him: "Why, during the golden age of stone lithography, with such print makers as Prang, and Currier & Ives,

1. *Bernhard von Schubert with progressive display in his conference room at Klingenberg Litho.*

2. *Klingenberg Logo and Coat of Arms showing date of inception (1570) and date of "Privileges" from the Prince (Feb. 1676)*

were cigar labels so far superior in quality and workmanship using up to 22 colors?" George nailed it down simply: "The cigar makers had the most money."

When you take the time to analyze that answer, it certainly makes sense. Currier & Ives' motto was: "We sell cheap prints." Yet here was a fiercely competitive (cigar) industry, making big profits. But with hundreds of new manufacturers coming along every month, working out of their basements, garages and back rooms, each had to find ways to make his product stand out from the rest. The label on the inside of the cigar box was, of course, the forerunner of what we now call "point of purchase" advertising, as the box sat open in the display case. So the cigar maker wanted a strong and attractive image to promote his brand.

Also important to the cigar manufacturer was the fact that only 55% of the public was literate. This meant that the *picture* was most important to the cigar maker wanting to promote his brand. Sadly enough, some things haven't changed much in the last 100 years!

I have provided a list of lithographers and label brokers whose names you will see on some of the labels that you acquire. However, for many of them, cigar labels did not contribute a major portion of their income. In spite of the fact that the 1899 directory of lithographers lists 410 plants in 29 states, by the early 1900's fewer than a dozen lithographers specialized in cigar labels and

3. *Calvert ad seen in a 19th Century Detroit directory.*

4. *19th Century Stone artists at Klingenberg Litho in Germany—courtesy of Bernhard and Bina von Schubert.*

aggressively pursued this part of the marketplace.

Some of the most outstanding labels you will discover from the "gilded age" were produced by Schlegel Litho, Schwencke Litho (which was bought out by Moehle around 1908, and became the American Colortype in 1928), Louis E. Neuman, Schmidt Litho, and American Litho, which was a consolidation of four major lithographers, finally becoming Consolidated Litho, the printing giant that absorbed American Litho and a host of others.

C. B. Henschel of Milwaukee and A. C. Henschel of Chicago are two names appearing on labels quite frequently. But they were actually label brokers, and used various lithographers for their stock, including German lithographers, whose bright gold leafing stood out in a Henschel Sample Book.

Cincinnati, with its German heritage, had a number of great lithographers, but when most people think of them, the name that comes to mind is Strobridge who was famous for circus posters. Progess Litho, started by Charles H. Klein, produced a variety of memorable artworks, including cigar labels. Mr. Klein is now 80 years old, and says he is still working seven days a week.

F. M. Howell of Elmira, New York, went after the low end of the market, selling inexpensive

5. Flatbed presses at Klingenberg–courtesy of Bernhard and Bina von Schubert.

6. Warehouseman at Klingenberg with bundles of cigar labels–courtesy of Bernhard and Bina von Schubert.

photomechanically produced labels for the small "Mom & Pop" cigar makers. His company worked out of the same building for over 100 years, and is still in business!

Howell was willing to sell in very small quantities, and even gave "exclusives" to certain dealers on specific labels. From an artistic standpoint, the Howell labels were quite mediocre, but they did produce some unique and sometimes humorous subjects. So from a collector's viewpoint, it would certainly be worthwhile to have a few samples from this lithographer who was an important supplier to one segment of the cigar industry.

There are examples of outstanding cigar labels produced by lithographers whose specialties were in other areas. One such example is Calvert Litho of Detroit, which was recently honored by the Education Department of the Detroit Institute of Art. A display of Calvert artworks toured Michigan's museums for an entire year, with excellent attendance at every stop. Calvert is probably recognized by museums and collectors mostly because of their production of the beautiful Ferry Seed posters and catalogues, which were equal in design and workmanship to the best cigar labels.

With a few exceptions like the *Lyra* cigar label, Calvert cigar labels are rather rare. Such blockbuster labels as *Fellow Citizen* (showing Grant and Lee), *Farragut* (showing Admiral Farragut in

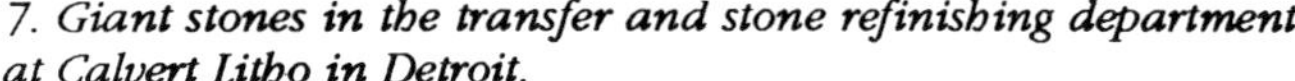

7. Giant stones in the transfer and stone refinishing department at Calvert Litho in Detroit.

8. Giant paper curing room at Calvert Litho.

battle scenes), and *La Rochelle* (featuring Cardinal Richelieu of France) are getting very hard to find. Calvert's outstanding artists catered to a continuing public taste for the style of art popularized by the Dusseldorf Academy.

In 1988, I had the privilege of touring the facilities of the Klingenberg Litho Company in Detmold, Germany. Although the main plant and offices have been moved for expansion purposes by their present owners, The Gundlach Group, a large conglomerate producing everything related to the graphic arts from executive gifts to calendars to cigar boxes and book publishing, they still respect and treasure all of the original artifacts from this historic printing company started in 1570!

As you walk into this modern establishment with all the latest technology of the 80's, you will see that the walls are decorated with cigar labels, posters, and other examples of their craftsmanship created during the golden age of stone lithography. Their conference room also has a display on the wall comprised of an actual litho stone, a disassembled progressive showing every color and registration step plus the final finished product which is the cigar label from the Garcia y Vega Co. (which is still in business). There is also a detailed explanation of every step involved, so their conference room wall boasts a better and more comprehensive exhibit of the stone litho process than I have ever seen in any museum.

The owners of Gundlach, Bernhard and Bina von Schubert, in spite of all their responsibilities running six divisions, have created an archive of all the surviving stones (and there are thousands) plus the label books, progressives and original art that has survived.

Surprisingly, Klingenberg survived the heavy bombing by the British in 1944, but sadly enough, thieves in the 1980's realizing the great value of these historical artworks, stole thousands of cigar labels and posters, many of them surfacing in the United States recently.

In an effort to keep the unique craft alive, the von Schuberts have launched a limited program of producing a modest amount of posters and calendars (using the original stones) which are being sold as executive gifts at very high prices.

This collection, which is undoubtedly the largest and most complete archive of stones, labels, and other artworks in the world, is being preserved at great expense by the von Schuberts in an effort to show future generations the complete history of stone lithography and never let it die.

9. *Stone storage racks at Calvert Litho.*

10. *Finishing department at Calvert Litho, the last step on these labels.*

It is quite fitting that the Klingenberg coat of arms *(pictured)* motto is *Saxa Loquuntus* or "Stones Speak". Although it is generally accepted that the death knell of Stone Lithography was in the 1920's when the new photomechanical process captured the lion's share of the market, Klingenberg Company records show that they were still using stones on special projects up until 1963! In my travels to Edinburgh, Scotland, I also was privileged to have interviewed Sid Johnston, an old-timer from Bartholemew Litho in that city who told me he was still working on stone flat-bed presses until the mid-1950's, again, for special projects demanding extremely high quality art.

Litho artists of the "Gilded Age" were an elite group, many arriving at work wearing top hats and white gloves, symbols of status as well as of their obsession with neatness and cleanliness in the craft. Just as many art collectors can spot the distinctive styles of their favorite artists, e.g., Winslow Homer, Benjamin West or Thomas Nast, I'm sure that many of you will be able to recognize a Calvert, a Schlegel or an O. L. Schwencke label from the artist's style. However, that method of identifying label lithographers might be more difficult for labels produced after 1920, because financial concerns encouraged many artists to become free-lancers, supplying a number of different lithographers throughout New York and Philadelphia. This eliminated a large payroll overhead for the lithographer, and also allowed the artist to create in his own environment, without a supervisor looking over his shoulder.

Lithographers of today, with all their new technology, are still in awe of the workmanship exhibited by the lithographers of the Gilded Age. Major corporations, including 3M and Mead Paper, regularly use cigar labels as executive awards, as does the Craftsman's Guild-International Printing House Craftsmen.

The following list contains the names of some of the lithographers and label brokers whose names may appear on labels for sale or in your collection. If no lithographer's name appears on the cigar label, it was at the request of the cigar maker, who didn't want his competitors to know where he was getting such great art work.

There were many mergers and acquisitions among this group in the period between 1880-1920. Some are obvious, as in the case of Thomas H. Heffron becoming Heffron & Phelps. The largest merger was the formation of the American Litho Company, formed by the merger of Schumacher & Etlinger, Witsch & Schmitt, Geo. Harris & Sons and F. Heppenheimer Sons.

American Label Company	New York
G.M. Boyd & Company	New York
Calvert Litho	Detroit
Cole Litho	Chicago
A. C. Henschel Company	Chicago
C. B. Henschel Company	Milwaukee
Schmitt & Company	New York
Witsch & Schmitt	New York
Schmidt & Company	New York & Chicago
Schwencke & Pfitzmayer	New York
O. L. Schencke	Brooklyn, NY
Moehle Litho	New York & Chicago
American Colortype	Chicago
Thomas H. Heffron	New York
Heffron & Phelps	New York
A. Ward Phelps	New York
Johns & Company	Cleveland
Otis Litho	Cleveland
Central Litho	Cleveland
Schumacher & Etlinger	New York & Chicago
Heppenheimer & Mauer	New York
F. Heppenheimer Sons	New York & Chicago
Conover Engraving & Printing	Coldwater, MI
Kreft Label & Printing	St. Louis
Guenther & Mueller	St. Louis
J. Guenther & Company	St. Louis
George S. Harris	Philadelphia
George S. Harris & Sons	Phila., NY & Chicago
Krueger & Braun	New York
Louis C. Wagner	New York
Sheip & Vandergrift	Philadelphia
Louis E. Neuman & Company	New York
Koelle-Mueller Label Company	St. Louis
F. M. Howell Company	Elmira, NY
Geo. Schlegel Litho	New York
Schlegel Litho	New York
Western Label Company	Milwaukee
Western Label and Supply	Leavenworth, KS
Moller, Kokeritz & Company	New York
Lancaster Litho	Lancaster, PA
T. A. Myers & Company	York, PA
E. Steffens Litho	New York
Eckstein & Hoffman Litho	New York

Wm. M. Donaldson Company	Cincinnati
Petre, Schmidt & Bergman	New York
Chicago Box Company	Chicago
Stecher Litho Company	New York
George S. Harris & Son	New York
Charles A. Wulff	New York
Hatch Litho Company	New York
Stahl & Jaeger	New York
H. Hoklas & Sons	Peoria, IL
New York Label Pub. Company	New York
Baltimore Litho	Baltimore
Isaac Friedenwald Litho	Baltimore
Maryland Litho	Baltimore
A. Hoen & Company	Richmond, VA
Heywood, Strasser & Voigt	New York
William Steiner & Sons	New York
Kaufman-Passbach-Voice	New York
Passbach-Voice	New York
Eastern Colortype	New York
H. H. Doehler & Company	New York
Sackell & Wilhelms Litho Co.	New York
Ackert Company	Cincinnati
Central Litho	Chicago
Cosack & Company	Buffalo
Donaldson Bros.	New York
Progress Litho	Cincinnati
Knight & Company	Cincinnati
J. H. Keithly	Cincinnati
Geo. F. Lashler	Philadelphia
Shober & Carqueville	Chicago
Seifert & Schneffel	Milwaukee
Albert Weise	Philadelphia
Wiegang & Frank	Germany
Gerhard & Heymanns	Germany
Klingenberg Litho	Germany
American Litho	New York
Consolidated Litho	New York
W. A. Shine	San Francisco
Mensing & Stecher	Rochester
Courier Litho	Buffalo
Michigan Litho	Grand Rapids
Bartholemew Litho	Scotland

COLLECTING CIGAR ART

hile serving for the past few years as an officer of Mensa (an organization dedicated to the study of human intelligence), I have had access to thousands of studies, grants and surveys on subjects ranging from the average I.Q.'s of doctors and attorneys (much lower than you might guess!) to indicators of giftedness in children. Along with such things as myopia, left-handness, love of chocolate and extreme allergies is, believe it or not, collecting! So, collectors, if you started at an early age collecting bottle caps, cigar bands, rocks, coins or baseball cards, statistics prove that you probably have an above average I.Q.! Here, for my above-average audience, is a look at how the hobby collecting got started.

Although information is scarce about the collecting habits of very early civilizations, there is enough data to indicate that collecting was a virtual obsession in some of the early cultures. When King Tut's tomb was opened, one of the first discoveries was his personal collection of beautifully carved whips and canes, inlaid with gold, which is now on display at the Cairo Museum.

Important collections of conquered countries were top priorities as spoils of war, one of the earliest examples being the tons of booty taken from Greece by the Romans. Though it was once commonly believed that the Romans were the first civilizations to collect on a grand scale, the Greeks preceeded them by more than a century. However, once the flow of art and collectibles began to reach Rome, at the height of the Roman Empire, collecting became a major activity.

Julius Caesar was the ultimate collector of his time. Whatever anyone else collected, he wanted, and his collections included coins, gems, cameos, works in gold and silver, fossils in amber, mosaic tables and books and manuscripts. After his death, his books and manuscripts were catalogued and made available to the public, and so was born the first public library.

Leap-frogging over a few centuries, we see evidence that collecting was an early interest in America. One of the most notable American collectors was Thomas Jefferson, who amassed a collection of over 9,000 books. Because of his interest in Natural History, Jefferson also commissioned Lewis and Clark to gather hundreds of fossil specimens from Kentucky.

Wealthy men such as J.P. Morgan and William Randolph Hearst went to great lengths to build their collections. Hearst started at the age of ten to collect stamps and coins, and graduated to clocks, rugs, cigarette lighters, the bed owned by Cardinal Richilieu and a Spanish Castle which he had shipped to California stone by stone and rebuilt in San Simeon!

Today's tycoons are a bit more sophisticated in their collecting, but the same drive and intensity that made them successful in business is apparent in their collecting. A good example is Malcomb Forbes, Sr., well known as the Chairman of Forbes Magazine, an honorable and energetic individual, an avid balloonist, who crossed Russia on a motorcycle while in his sixties. Not so widely known is his spectacular collection of Fabergé Eggs, nor his vast array of lead toy soldiers which is rated as the best in the world.

I saw the intensity, drive, and desire of Malcolm Forbes as a dedicated collector in 1983, when I acquired a rare cigar label proof of a gentleman with the title of "*Lord Forbes.*" I sent it, framed, to Mr. Forbes along with a friendly note saying that if he could tell me who this man was, and what his relationship was with the Forbes' clan, he could have it free! Here's where the dedicated collector's genes take charge!

Mr. Forbes commissioned his son Chris to track down all early engravings and paintings of Forbes relatives, and in a short time the portrait was found hanging in the dining room in Forbes' castle in Aberdeenshire, Scotland.

Chris sent me not only a photo of the portrait, but a complete biography of the man, who had an outstanding military career, lived to the age of 78 (amazing in those times) and was responsible for the planting of 6,888,360 trees on the Forbes estate from 1805-1814. Ecologists should honor him today, but we'll never know why he was chosen to grace a cigar label.

Author's Note: If you'd like to have something in common with Malcomb Forbes, Sr., he also owns the following cigar labels: *Paid in Full, Bank Note, Record Bond, Bankable, First National, Dime Bank and Gold Dollar* as I recall.

In the early 20th Century, the collecting of cigar bands boomed, but cigar label collections were virtually non-existent. I believe label collecting began with the actions of resourceful early band collectors like Joe Hruby, whom I mention in the Cigar Band Chapter. Not satisfied with just searching sidewalks and gutters for bands, they began to write to cigar manufacturers for samples of their bands.

Since the manufacturers were always looking for new avenues of exposure and trying to create "brand awareness"among buyers, they responded to the requests by sending entire "sets" including the bands, inner and outer labels and sometimes even the trim. The young collectors were ecstatic with their new acquisitions of bands. But they had no format for the display of labels, so those were simply stored in boxes or scrapbooks, separate from the bands. Little did they know that in the near future the labels would be worth 5,000% more than the bands.

In spite of multi-page color articles written in *Fortune* magazine in 1933, *Esquire* magazine in

1949, and *Eros* magazine in 1962, very few people in this country collected cigar labels. But by the mid-1970's, things began to change rapidly. People known in the antique trade as "diggers and pickers"–individuals who are on the alert for any type of "old" items abandoned in old buildings and warehouses–started finding bundles of labels in some of the old box factories and cigar factories in Eastern Pennsylvania. But the diggers had a dilemma: they knew these labels were old because of the dates on packages, as well as the time the factories had gone out of business; but the labels didn't look old. And to impress antique and flea market dealers, paper ephemera had to be dirty, stained and generally old looking. The dealers obviously didn't know how to use a magnifying glass to detect the unreproducible style of the stipple artist, and they wouldn't buy the labels because they looked too new.

What these poor souls didn't know was that the labels represented the high water mark of the lithographers' craft. The finest inks, top quality rag paper, and clay and casein coatings used would keep them looking great until the year 3000!

In spite of the refusal of most dealers to accept these beautiful prints, some bundles of labels did make it to the flea market tables, and that's where the art dealers first saw them. From Brimfield in Massachusetts to the Rose Bowl in California, art dealers with magnifying glasses in hand, started gobbling up as many of these pristine chromolithographs as they could find. They framed them attractively and created a whole new "Country Store" look, which has been growing ever since.

Starting in 1979, when a story about Cigar Label Collecting hit the front page of the *Wall Street Journal*, interest developed in areas the antique dealers would never have dreamed of. Department stores from Bloomingdale's in New York to Dilliard's in Arizona featured massive displays. Ethan Allen stores, major galleries like Merrill-Chase in Chicago and A.B. Clossen in Cincinnati devoted entire walls to these spectacular 12-to 22-color chromolithographs. More importantly, Fortune 500 companies like Mead Paper, 3M Company and North American Phillips started giving them as executive gifts to all their most important clients. These giant companies got the message that the early discoverers missed: they weren't selling cigar labels, they're selling Art, History and Americana.

Once the collector is hooked on these beautiful labels which he has framed on his wall, he wants more and more, and, running out of wall space, he next turns to building albums. This was my route. Like Caesar, I wanted them *all*, but I realized that was an impossible task. So I started to build albums by subject matter: famous men, women, animals, Negroes, cowboys and Indians, etc. This has at least allowed me to have a diversity in subject matter in a medium that I love, without needing to have it *all*.

Looking at cigar label art as a historian and educator, I felt it was necessary to have representations of each laborious step needed to produce these beautiful works of art, so I have included proofs, progressives, sample labels and even a few litho stones in my collection.

My advice to the collector is to collect what you like; but, to add to the collection's intrinsic value, it would be wise not to pinpoint an area that is too specific, like financial labels, or Uncle Sam, for example, because that would result in a rather thin album. Since there were so many lithographers at the turn of the century, you might specialize in a few of them, and have a pretty substantial album of, for example, Schlegel or Schwencke, Heppenheimer or Schmidt. Another unique approach I've seen was to collect only 4" x 4" outside labels, which for some reason are not as plentiful as the 6" x 9" inner labels. But they have all of that great artwork condensed into a smaller space, and can be stored in very small albums.

One collector I know collects only samples, and is perfectly willing to trade away spectacular labels that are not samples in order to enhance his own collection. John Grossman, who is an internationally recognized design artist, tries to obtain examples of all the art created, not only the large "6 x 9" inner label, but also the trim and outer labels which in many cases had design ties with the main label.

As you can see, there are many options. The time is ripe, since there are hundreds of dealers out there who neither appreciate nor understand the value of these outstanding examples of the lost art of chromolithography, and you, with your keen eye, and the knowledge acquired in this book, can still snap them up at bargain prices!

DATING LABELS

Often it is difficult to date labels exactly, because a cigar manufacturer would sometimes take advantage of volume pricing and order 100,000 labels, which might last for a generation. Someone may tell you that a brand was still seen in the stores after World War II, even though the labels were actually produced in 1916! Tobacco leaf journals show registration dates, but the only known complete set is owned by the University of South Florida. Without access to the set, and barring the date actually appearing on the label, your best hope of dating labels is in the following benchmarks.

Labels produced before 1890 were almost always created by the crayon method graphically shown in the chapter on lithography. Also, since embossing wasn't incorporated until the early 1890's, a non-embossed label revealing the crayon method definitely falls into the time frame of the 1870's to the 1890's; some stippling would possibly be evident towards the end of that period.

Another area of identification for such early labels is the use of finely grooved paper, which has the appearance of cloth. This paper acted as a safeguard to the lithographer; if one of the runs on the press was slightly out of registration, it would absorb any slight mistake in its grooved surface. The use of this paper was discontinued with the introduction of embossing, which required much heavier coated stock.

The "golden age" of labels started with the advent of gilding and embossing in the early 1890's. If cigar labels were the high-water mark of the advertising illustrator's art, the period from 1890 to 1920 was the high-water mark of cigar label art.

Fierce competition led the thousands of cigar makers to give virtually a blank check to the lithographers to create better, more elaborate artworks than their competitors. Thus the lithographers were motivated to generate some of the most unbelievable examples of chromolithographic art ever to be produced. The labels of this period displayed the abilities of the stipple artist to create spectacular shading and tones, by using up to 22 separate registrations (see example in chapter on Lithography).

By the middle of the 1920's, two events occurred: cigar sales were finally overtaken by cigarettes, causing the cigar makers to do some belt-tightening; and the four color process (photomechanical) was adopted, eliminating the stone litho artists and bringing to the marketplace cheaper, but far less attractive labels. Although the cheaper photomechanically produced labels continued to be embossed, it was impossible to duplicate the labels produced in the previous three decades.

The example of the labels shown in the lithography chapter will assist you in identifying them. But once you have been able to compare them with your own eyes, you probably won't ever need a magnifying glass.

SEARCHING FOR LABELS

For cigar label collectors, as for most hunters, the chase is often more invigorating than the kill. There are hundreds of stories about collectors going to unbelievable extremes to obtain that "one" item they needed for their collection. On the other hand, the most painful memories, at least to me, are of the times when something gets away because you were not aggressive enough. There are a number of ways to track down and acquire great labels, and to have fun doing it. One of the obvious ways is to search for ads in the various antique publications, to see what is being offered by the dealers. But beware of the ads that surface from time to time, offering "100 labels for $45" or "50 labels for $25." This is one of the oldest scams in existence, with slight variations.

I guarantee you will receive the promised number of labels. But in all our mystery shopping escapades, we have found that the individual making the offer is cleaning out his scrap barrel; he will send you a couple of fairly common but nice pictorial labels, along with an assortment of bow-wows that you would be ashamed to put in your collection. The results are that you have grossly overpaid for a couple of common labels, and he has finally gotten rid of some of his junk.

If a dealer is reputable, knows his market, and is proud of what he has to offer, he should provide you with a full pictorial brochure, or at least provide you with Xerographic copies so you that you can decide whether you like the style or the subject matter. Just a listing of titles is not enough, because labels from the late 1920's to 1930's were quite inferior to the images done at the turn of the century. For example, Calvert Litho produced an outstanding *First National* label around 1908, showing a majestic building with great detail in the bricks, a horse carriage, old auto and even a streetcar. Decades later, a number of lithographers produced labels that simply said *First National*,

with no other pictorial graphics. If the catalog list in your hand just said *First National* for $6.00 you might think you're getting the great one at a bargain price, what a disappointment it would be to receive the other one, and try to return it!

There are some very good paper dealers out there, aggressively uncovering new finds. It's up to you to test them and see if they can deliver new and exciting images with some degree of regularity, and it's up to them to earn your patronage. The old cliche still holds: The customer is always right!

As a collector of many forms of antiquarian graphics, I have made some of my greatest discoveries among non-art dealers. For example, an antique dealer who "specializes" in glass or furniture may buy out an estate. If he is worth his salt, he will buy everything in the building, not only the pieces that are important to him, and will consider any money earned from the ancillary items as "found money."

In many cases, a dealer who has a small pile of labels, or an old album full of them, has no idea what to charge for them. To avoid looking unprofessional, he puts them under the counter or "on the back burner" so to speak. So I strongly recommend that if you are making the rounds of antique shops or shows and see only glass or furniture, you should ask, "Do you have any old prints or advertising artworks?" Four times out of five you may get nothing but a blank stare, but the fifth time... jackpot!

I learned a great lesson a while back when I was attending an important showing of cigar art put on by the University of South Florida at Tampa. My roommate at this three day function was Dr. Tony Hyman, tobaccianna expert and author of *Cash For Undiscovered Treasures*. Since Sunday morning was open for both of us, we decided to drive north to a giant flea market and see what treasures we could find. Arriving at 6 a.m., to be the first ones in (very important point), we split up, agreeing to meet at the car at noon. I used my usual method of walking down the middle of the aisles, trusting my peripheral vision to spot the bright colors only stone lithos seem to maintain.

At noon, Tony was waiting with arms full of treasures, including rare postcards of the old tobacco parades in Ybor City to great tobacco tins including one with a hockey player on it! He had charged out of the starting gate and talked to every booth holder, with the opening line: "Do you have any tobacco-related items?" I certainly didn't strike out in my foray, but I should have remembered a line that I always used with my students: the only stupid question is the one that's never asked!

Another non-typical avenue for digging up cigar art is through coin dealers. After the big gold and silver boom in the early 80's, many coin dealers realized that they already were selling collectibles, so why not expand their base? Today, when you go into a coin shop that has survived, you will very likely see displays of old comic books, baseball cards and in some cases fine art posters, old advertising and–cigar labels! These people know what sells!

As I mentioned in the chapter on collecting, department stores, art galleries and print shops features cigar labels along with other original "Country Store" items. You will also see cigar art offered from time to time in some of the more prestigeous mail order catalogs, at very high prices and very beautifully framed.

Now that we have looked at some of the retail avenues for finding cigar labels, what's wrong with searching for the mother lode? That's right, why shouldn't *you* discover an old cigar factory, litho firm or box company with stacks of labels stuck in a corner or attic? Not only could you dramatically enhance your own collection, you could also probably net a few thousand dollars for all your extras, or use them as trade to expand your collection. But how does one go about finding such a mother lode? It's a lot easier than you might guess.

The statement "everything you ever wanted to know is in the library" is very true. You just have to know how to use the library. Most main libraries have stored away all their old city directories, or have them on microfilm, going back to their days of charter.

Pick out a directory from the period around 1900-1910, and look for the listings of cigar makers (you may be surprised at how many there are) or boxmakers. Then work your way forward to see when they went out of business, or if they became a tobacco and candy distributors which may still be in business. Take a current phone book and see if there are any people in town with the same name that you can call to find out if there is a relationship. (Less common names are easiest to pinpoint, of course: Weisenstein Cigar Co. vs. Jones Cigar Co.)

Small town people are usually very friendly, and often volunteer a lot more information than you expected: "No, that's not our side of the family, they have a daughter who is still living and her name is Johnson. Let me find her number for you." Once you find Mrs. Johnson, explain what you are looking for. In many cases the party will say that everything was destroyed or thrown away, but at least one time in twenty your heart will flutter when you hear, "Oh yes, we've got boxes of that old stuff out in our barn!"

One extremely successful search mission of mine was the small town of Belmont, Ohio, which listed seven cigar factories in 1905. I found two separate hoards that had never been touched since 1929! Unfortunately, because of all my other responsibilities, I don't get out on the road as much as I did, but in spite of my present work load, I try to plan at least three or four trips per year. It's really great therapy, and, quite rewarding.

For another source of information, you might try to acquire a copy of an old government directory of cigar makers, listed by tax number. Since the tobacco trade has always been taxed and closely policed by the Federal Government, these directories were published showing each cigar maker's assigned tax number, which had to appear on each box, no matter how large or small the factory was. The directories are broken down by state, with each taxing district listing the cities and towns in their jurisdiction. A city like Cincinnati or Philadelphia will take up two or three pages, listing 100 or more cigar makers per page. A cigar maker who had a very low assigned number would proudly display it right on his main label; for example the *Sanchez and Haya* label proudly proclaims they were assigned Factory #1 in Tampa.

Surprisingly, some of the most remote and unlikely small towns imaginable will list from three to twelve cigar "factories" at that town time. Those are the places where you will most likely strike gold. Collectors are an ingenious and creative lot and I am sure some of you will make some spectacular finds in the years to come.

VALUES & RARITY

It has always been amusing and, sometimes sad the way values are assigned to collectibles and antiques by individuals who have not done any research or have any specific benchmarks to measure by. The IRS interpretation of fair market value is, quite simply, what two individuals at arms length are willing to sell for and to pay. This is not an affront to professional appraisers who now have computer programs loaded with past auction and sales results at their fingertips, and, taking condition, quantity available, and a number of other unique features into consideration, are usually pretty darn close on a lot of items. Actually, most appraisers, including myself are extremely pleased when an item goes for much higher than the appraisal because that is an obvious indication of an increase in interest in that item.

My displeasure is with the individual who conducts a "one man survey" in his own little microcosm and says "there's a million of them out there" after he has seen just a few surfacing in different areas and is worried if he buys one that there is "a million of them out there." Even more ludicrous is the individual who, for example sees an original Audubon in a dusty old shop in New Orleans for $40.00, yet 500 dealers around the country are selling original Audubons for $400! He is convinced that Audubons are worth $40.00!

That is what has always worried me about price guides. Mainly what are the credentials of the individuals assigning these prices, and how old is this guide? Since, if you will recall in the late seventies, coin prices changed before the ink was dry on the "new" guides. Fortunately, cigar art prices have been fairly easy to track, and, have shown much steadier growth than most mutual funds.

Every auction I have participated in since 1983 has set new record highs for certain subject matters, and, the more effective dealers have reported to me through the years as to "price-resistance levels" which also are rising. A humorous note was from an old-time dealer, who, in the 1970's told me: "No label on this earth is worth more than $7.00!" Three years later, I asked how much he wanted for a sports subject label and he said: "The best I can do for you Joe, is $400.00." I reminded him of his prediction of the $7.00 ceiling, but the only satisfaction I got was that he promised not to prophecize anymore.

What I have attempted to do for you in this publication is to assign value *ranges* based upon quantity, desirability, quality of artwork, and subject matter. If a label has been assigned one star(*), the quantities in existence are usually over 5,000 and can be acquired usually for under $10.00. If the label has been assigned two stars (**), then its desirability has been enhanced by either the subject matter or quality of artwork, exists in quanitities of less than 5,000 and has a range or $10-$25. For those labels with three stars (***), you are now getting into an area of less than 1,000 in existance and a fairly great subject matter or artwork. Three star labels should command from $25-$75. Four stars (****), is the best rating I can assign which would fall in the price category of over $75.00, but remember that figure is $75 and up, and auction records show many, many labels going for $100-$400 with great regularity. Some very unique examples in this book are the *Hans Wagner* and *Little Niggers* at over $1,000, *Frontier* at $400 and *Fellow Citizens* at $150. Besides their great artwork and subject matter, four star labels are *extremely* rare, with only a handful of each surviving.

Interestingly enough, many of the high prices realized at auctions have not been from cigar label collectors for these four star labels, but, as in the case of the *Hans Wagner*, you have what is called a "cross-collectible".

The first *Hans Wagner* I offered at auction went to a baseball card dealer who knew the value of Hans Wagner as a hot subject matter in his market place. There was a temporary stigma applied to the *Hans Wagner* for awhile, since although only 18 are known to exist, an unscrupulous dealer who had acquired six of them, told each buyer he sold to that, "It was the only one known to exist." This made no sense whatsoever, since one, he should have known that advanced collectors discuss their new acquistions, and two, 18 of an item in a country of this size is still super-rare and would not really affect the price in the long run.

Another example of a cross-collectible was the *Lime Kiln Club* label depicting a raucous meeting of negroes which went to a black collector for $310.00. Undoubtedly, new records will be set in the future, and new discoveries will pop out of abandoned warehouses from time to time.

But what is most interesting is the fact that all financial gurus say that collectibles fare best during times of inflation, or at least climb evenly with inflation, and yet, cigar label art has grown steadily in value over the past eight years with virtually no inflation! I certainly don't want to see another inflation spiral like the late seventies, but I now have much greater respect for my cigar label collection if it does happen!

MISCELLANEOUS GENRES

After zeroing in on major and minor "themes" used on cigar labels which could obviously be broken down further and further, I felt that the best way to give you an overview of the full spectrum of subjects was in this type of chapter. Considering the thousands of images available to me for publication, I decided to not impose my taste by conducting a one-man survey, but use all the data available to me through dealers and auctions as to which labels had the most appeal. In some cases, little or no information is available on a label, but that certainly should not demean its appeal or collectibility. Obviously, the number of images that can be shown in a book like this is limited, so I apologize if your favorites do not appear.

1. *Abe Martin:* This was a famous Indiana cartoon character, philosopher created by Kin Hubbard, who was born in Bellefontaine, Ohio in 1868. Abe Martin was syndicated in over 300 newspapers. Like Will Rogers, Hubbard's humor was never malicious and was proud that he lived in a time when "nobody was afraid to drink at the town pump." Abe Martin was one of the earliest cartoon characters to appear on a cigar label right after the "Yellow Kid."
2. *Alvara:* attractive art-nouveau style label created for the J.C. Alvarez Company of Philadelphia.
3. *Africora:* another confusing title by American Litho featuring a pretty girl in Spanish garb with a West Indies backdrop.
4. *Aristocrat:* unknown artistocrats cameoed on each side of a Cuban street with Moro Castle in the background. Created for the C.E. Bair Company by Consolidated Litho.
5. *Bacchante:* extremely popular label among collectors partially because it was featured in the March 1933 Fortune Magazine story.
6. *Belvedere:* excellent use of only one color and gold embossing by the Ace Cigar Company of Buffalo, New York.
7. *Brick House:* popular Tampa brand owned by the M & N Cigar Company and produced by Consolidated Litho.

8. *Castle Hall:* outstanding artwork of unknown overgrown castle in Cuba. Early versions were purported to have originated in Cuba, but records show it being produced in the U.S. by Petre, Schmidt & Bergmann of New York.
9. *Chicago Hand Made:* beautiful early 20th Century skyline of Chicago created by Schlegel Litho.
10. *The Clown:* extremely rare label created for the W.F. Gabrio Company by Schlegel Litho.
11. *Columbia Dome:* the Frieman Cigar Company of St. Louis created this for the Columbian exposition held there.
12. *Custom House:* originally created by the Jacob Stahl, Jr. Company. The brand was taken over by American Cigar Company in 1902, featuring custom houses in Chicago, St. Louis, Boston, New York and Memphis.
13. *Diamond Crown:* popular brand of the M & N Cigar Company showing three major monarchs from the 1800's. We can only guess that one was Peter the Great and the Queen was most likely Victoria, but this artist was not a realist.
14. *Darby & Joan:* Tampa cigar brand featuring older couple drinking, possibly they were fictional book characters.
15. *Don Nieto:* another good example of using only black and gold for maximum effect. This was produced for the Don Nieto Cigar Company in 1923.
16. *Duke de Oro:* "Duke of Gold" another Spaniard produced for the Pent Bros. of Philadelphia by Calvert Litho. Calvert's artists were not afraid to experiment with a lot of colors and came up with this blockbuster piece of lithography.
17. *Duo-Art:* nameless Spanish-looking nobleman. Good art created by Schlegel Litho.
18. *Echo Bay:* very early art probably produced by Harris or Heppenheimer.
19. *El Biscayne:* label promoting Miami, "The World's Winter Playground."
20. *El Pensivo:* scene featuring pensive female being comforted with music by a friend. Created by Calvert Litho.
21. *Engagement:* very popular roaring twenties brand created for the F.X. Smith Company of McSherrystown, Pa.
22. *Epco:* 1920's brand featuring Egyptian beauty.
23. *Exposition:* 1892 label honoring the famous Columbian Exposition in Chicago, created by Schlegel Litho.
24. *First National:* probably one of *the* best labels created by Calvert Litho. Outstanding work and detail on the building, but also great detail on the street car, horse and buggy, car and people. This label is coveted by collectors from many fields, including coin dealers and financial ephemera collectors.
25. *Garcia Mystery:* a Florida brand, but the cigar maker and lithographer are also a mystery.
26. *Ghost:* a great piece of work by Witsch and Schmidt but certainly not a "theme" label since it's the only one I have even seen featuring a ghost.
27. *Grey Horse:* excellent use of only three colors by the F.M. Howell Company although it is titled *Grey Horse,* it is actually a rendition of a statue of General James Outram who commanded the British forces in India in the 19th Century.
28. *Havana Post:* unique rendition of Havana newspaper dated May 29, 1904. Torn out section reveals the Moro lighthouse at Moro Castle.
29. *Havana Rope:* the Alfonso Rios Company chose another way to feature the famous Moro Castle.
30. *High Toned:* great artwork done by the Geo. Schlegel Litho Company for the Brucker & Boghien Cigar Company. This was one of the early efforts to associate cigar smoking with the upper classes.
31. *Ideolo:* great detailed artwork showing coats of arms and Roman figures. No data on lithographer or maker.
32. *Jano:* striking presentation and use of color for just another Spanish dancer, discovered in Buffalo, New York.
33. *Jewelo:* another striking approach showing a cavalier and farm girl.
34. *King Cotton:* created for the M.H. Sevis and Son Company in Spring Vale, Pennsylvania. This must have been popular with the cotton Growers' lobby, because I can't fathom any other promotional tie to cigars.
35. *Knickerbockers:* created for the Lewis Osterweis and Sons Company which started in New Haven, Conn. in 1860.
36. *La Coqueta:* early Heffron and Phelps Litho production showing Coquettish girl removing mask.

37. *La Festa:* Roman emperor with Vesuvius and Coliseum in background created in 1911 for the very large Saeger and Sons Cigar Company in Fremont, Nebraska.
38. *La Lunda:* outstanding example of German lithography and gold leafing imported by the C.B. Henschel Label Brokers from Milwaukee, Wisconsin.
39. *La Sciencia:* cigar makers even alluded to the Health Advantages of smoking their cigars. Calvert Litho of Detroit created this brand for the Minnesota Pharmaceutical Mfg. Company in St. Paul, which "backed this brand with their reputation."
40. *La Victoria:* Christopher Columbus was used many times on a variety of tobacco products since he was tied to its early use in Europe. This is probably one of the few that doesn't show Indians lurking in the bushes.
41. *Little Cousins:* possibly a vanity brand but no information could be found on this one.
42. *Little Knicks:* popular New York brand showing midgets (or poorly drawn children) in Knickerbocker outfits. The Statue of Liberty and Brooklyn Bridge appear in the background.
43. *Los Tres:* here is Columbus again, this time with the Indians in the bushes.
44. *Magnolia:* beautiful custom floral label created for the Phil D. Mayer and Son Company in New Orleans.
45. *Mostavana:* Calvert Litho created another outstanding claim this time by "Professor A, Nalyzer" attesting that they contain "more Havana Tobacco than any other 5¢ cigar."
46. *Nabob:* a turbaned potentate tried to add class to these very likely inferior cigars marked down to 2 for 5¢. This pricing is usually indicative of depression era cigars.
47. *Navy Ribbon:* another post-Spanish American War label looking for nautical buffs.
48. *Nordacs:* Viking image used by the Florida Cigar Company in Quincy, Florida.
49. *Old King Cole:* original Maxfield Parrish art created by the Geo. Schlegel Litho Company. This label has set new auction records every time it has appeared. A tin with this paper label went for over $1000.
50. *Old Well:* pastoral scene created for the H.E. Shaw Company by Geo. Schlegel Litho.
51. *Omar:* "The Nation's Sensation" *Omar* was an advisor to Mohammed the Prophet and was also a brand name for cigarettes. The label was produced by Consolidated Litho.
52. *O'San:* another Arabic scene with very unique design also created by Consolidated Litho.
53. *Paid In Full:* an extremely coveted label featuring cash, checks, stacks and bags of coins created by Geo. Schlegel Litho.
54. *Palace Court:* outstanding three dimensional effect created by Schlegel Litho artists.
55. *Pandora:* a brand belonging to the H.B. Grauley Cigar Company which used many different children on their labels. This one stumps me.
56. *Shoe Peg:* a brand of cigars that had a wooden peg in the end which eliminated snipping or biting. Their slogan: "Do not bite, pull out peg and light." I still don't know how the shoe fit in.
57. *Record Bond:* another very successful money related theme created by Consolidated Litho.
58. *Red Mill:* unique theme created 1897 by American Litho.
59. *Rigoletto:* popular brand created by the M & N Cigar Company of Tampa based on the character from the famous opera.
60. *Romance:* quality artwork created by Schlegel Litho for the Yocum Bros. Cigar Company.
61. *Royal Opera:* another Schlegel design, this time for the Spector Bros. in Chicago, Illinois.
62. *Salzburg:* Austrian Alps scene created by Consolidated Litho.
63. *Seal of Philadelphia:* Charles Seider Cigar in Philadelphia used this official looking seal to try to promote his cigars.
64. *Sir Loraine:* copyrighted in 1911, the Julius Bien Cigar Company probably had to pay a considerable price for this quality art. Lithographer is unknown.
65. *Snow Man:* extremely rare label produced by the Geo. Schlegel Litho Company, just like the *Ghost* brand, I have never seen a snowman used before to sell cigars. Any labels showing snow scenes, other than Christmas themes, are also quite unique.
66. *Spana Leo:* heraldic style label created for the San Telmo Cigar Company.
67. *Sophomore:* label depicting three temples of learning, Oxford, Yale, and AOH'nai for the Trans-Pacific Trading Company in Chicago. This brand of cigars was hand-made by the Blaine Stewart Cigar Company in Hicksville, Ohio. A very rare and coveted label.
68. *Student Prince:* beautiful label created for the M & N Cigar Company by Consolidated Litho. Besides the play, *Student Prince* is the name of the Heidelberg College Sports teams in Tiffin, Ohio.
69. *Tampa Life:* one of the most coveted Tampa labels found, produced by American Litho for the

Preston Cigar Company. This is the famous old Tampa Bay Hotel, which is now part of the University of Tampa.
70. *Treaty Bond:* high quality art produced by Schlegel Litho featuring the Louisiana Purchase along with Napoleon and Thomas Jefferson.
71. *Tuval:* great image of Roman gladiator produced for the Antonio Cigar Company of Tampa.
72. *Uncle Jake's Nickel Seegar:* "Five cents wurth o' dern good smokin" says cartoon character Uncle Jake. These cigars featuring another cartoon character were distributed by the Goldman Bros. in Corsicana, Texas.
73. *Upper Ten:* This was a designation given to the cream of society in New York. The "dude" or "swell" in the center was produced by Moehle Litho in Brooklyn, New York but the *Upper Ten* name was letterpressed in later. I have seen this label with other titles, so *Upper Ten* may not have survived very long.
74. *Vest Pocket:* popular image created by Consolidated Litho and even reproduced (very poorly) by a publisher trying to reproduce cigar labels. The reproductions are very easy to spot since they are larger in size than a cigar label and are poor quality photomechanical work.
75. *Western Bee:* another popular brand of the Saeger & Sons Cigar Company of Fremont, Nebraska produced by Schmidt Litho. The bunch of cigars takes on the appearance of a beehive.
76. *White Heather:* a Cuesta-Rey brand from Tampa which reads: "Awarded gold medal - San Francisco Exposition, 1915."
77. *Wizard:* great litho work and great subject matter. The Wizard in the dragon-emblazoned robe is causing the tobacco leaves to rise from the bales while the Black cat has every hair standing on end. An extremely coveted label.

1. Abe Martin **
2. Alvara **
3. Africora *

1.

3.

2.

*4. Aristocrat **
*5. Bacchante ***
*6. Belvedere **
*7. Brick House **
*8. Castle Hall **
*9. Chicago Hand Made ***

6.

BACCHANTE

5.

7.

BRICK HOUSE

8.

4.

ARISTOCRAT

9.

*10. The Clown *****
*11. Columbia Dome ****
*12. Custom House ****
*13. Diamond Crown ***
*14. Darby & Joan ***

10.

11.

12.

THE
CUSTOM HOUSE
CIGAR
CHICAGO
ST. LOUIS
NEW YORK
BOSTON
MEMPHIS
TRADE MARK TRANSFERRED BY JACOB STAHL, JR. & CO. TO AMERICAN CIGAR COMPANY, JANUARY, 1902.

13.

14.

*15. Don Nieto **
*16. Duke de Oro ****
*17. Duo-Art ***
*18. Echo Bay ***
*19. El Biscayne ***

15.

16.

17.

19.

18.

20. El Pensivo **
21. Engagement **
22. Epco **
23. Exposition ***
24. First National **

20.

21.

22.

23.

SMOKE EXPOSITION CIGARS

24.

FIRST NATIONAL

*25. Garcia Mystery **
*26. Ghost *****
*27. Grey Horse ***
*28. Havana Post ***

25.

26.

27.

28.

*29. Havana Rope **
*30. High Toned ***
*31. Ideolo ***
*32. Jano ****
*33. Jewelo **

30.

32.

29.

33.

31.

34.

34. *King Cotton* *
35. *Knickerbockers* *
36. *La Coqueta* **
37. *La Festa* **
38. *La Lunda* ***

35.

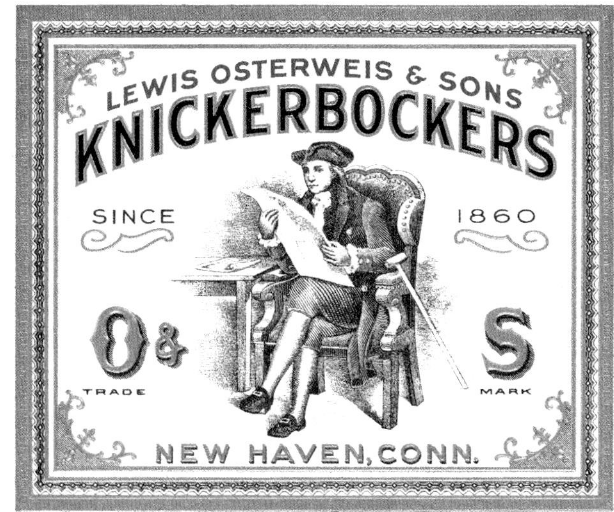

Lewis Osterweis & Sons
NEW HAVEN, CONN.

BE SURE THEY ARE OSTERWEIS' KNICKERBOCKERS

LEWIS OSTERWEIS & SONS KNICKERBOCKERS NEW HAVEN, CONN.

36.

37.

38.

*39. La Sciencia ****
*40. La Victoria ***
*41. Little Cousins **
*42. Little Knicks ***
*43. Los Tres ***

39.

41.

40.

42.

43.

*44. Magnolia ****
*45. Mostavana ***
*46. Nabob **
*47. Navy Ribbon ***
*48. Nordacs ***

45.

44.

47.

NAVY RIBBON

NOW 2 FOR 5¢

After all nothing satisfies like a good cigar

46.

EXTRA MILD NABOB LONG FILLER

48.

NORDACS

FLORIDA CIGAR CO., INC. QUINCY, FLA. NORDACS FLORIDA CIGAR CO., INC. QUINCY, FLA.

*49. Old King Cole *****
*50. Old Well ***
*51. Omar ***
*52. O'San ***
*53. Paid In Full ****

49.

52.

50.

51.

53.

54. Palace Court ***
55. Pandora *
56. Shoe Peg *
57. Record Bond **
58. Red Mill ***

54.

PANDORA

55.

56.

The One and only One Original Old Time
5¢
STRAIGHT
PEG
DO NOT BITE
PULL OUT PEG
AND LITE

ORIGINAL SHOE PEG OLD TIME

57.

RECORD BOND

58.

SMOKE RED MILL CIGARS

*59. Rigoletto **
*60. Romance ***
*61. Royal Opera ***
*62. Salzburg ***
*63. Seal of Philadelphia **

59.

60.

62.

61.

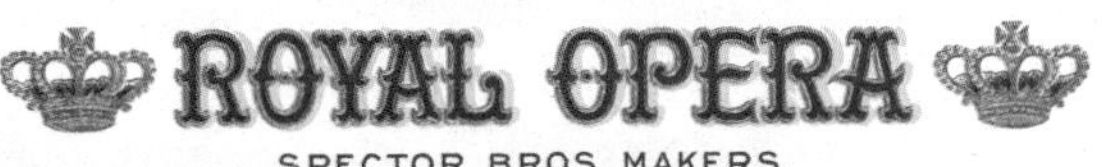

63.

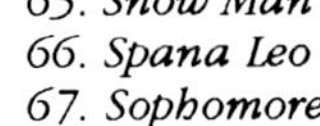

*64. Sir Loraine ***
*65. Snow Man *****
*66. Spana Leo **
*67. Sophomore ***

64.

65.

67.

66.

*68. Student Prince ***
*69. Tampa Life ****
*70. Treaty Bond ***

69.

68.

70.

71. *Tuval* **
72. *Uncle Jake's Nickel Seegar* **
73. *Upper Ten* **
74. *Vest Pocket* *

71.

73.

74.

VEST POCKET

UNCLE JAKE'S NICKEL SEEGAR

72.

*75. Western Bee **
*76. White Heather ***
*77. Wizard ***

75.

76.

77.

THEATER

Just as many of today's TV commercials use famous personalities to promote everything from diet foods to automobiles, the cigar industry used Theater personalities to promote some of their particular brands of cigars. On many of the theatrical labels you find, you will see the statement "By Permission" and then possibly a facsimile signature, on others you will see no such designation of permission. The archives of the Schlegel Litho did contain affidavits from such personalities as Lillian Russell and William Gillette giving their permission to use their names and images, but I am sure that as time progressed, some of the more aggressive label makers took their chances and hoped they wouldn't get sued.

Since most of the labels portraying theater personalities were usually very well done and at possibly great expense in an effort to please the entertainer, you could build a collection of theater related labels and have a very attractive and valuable collection.

1. *Lillian Russell*: famous singer and stage star. A number of newspaper articles reported that "Miss Russell smoked up to 50 cigars a day", no wonder she allowed her likeness on a label!
2. *William Gillette*: famous for his portrayal of Arthur Conan Doyle's "Sherlock Holmes."
3. *Ethel Barrymore*: famous female member of the Barrymore family whom most of you remember playing an elderly lady in the movies. The Schlegel Litho Company did an outstanding job of capturing her beauty in her early career.
4. *Irish Singer*: Dennis O'Sullivan, famous singer and actor born in San Francisco in 1868.
5. *Rudolph Valentino*: silent film star with vignettes showing him as a sheik and as a Spaniard. This label also bears his facsimile signature, but we'll never know if they had his permission or not.
6. *Kyra*: famous belly dancer who received much publicity during the early 20's about her "outrageous seductive dancing."
7. *Clint Ford*: famous New York actor who appeared frequently at the Star Theatre, considered the leading theater in America in the late 1800's.

8. *Arthur Donaldson*: early 1920's actor depicted in his famous role as the "Prince of Pilsen."
9. *Gabler's Judge*: New England actor Peter Gabler shown in his role as a judge.
10. *Lillian Ashley*: no traceable lithographer for this label, but they did appear to have her permission and the title was registered.
11. *Jean Valjean*: fictional star character in Victor Hugo's "Les Miserables."
12. *Three Twins*: here is a case where a popular play received recognition on a cigar label.
13. *Neil Burgess*: famous female impersonator with vignettes showing him in roles in "County Fair" and "Widow Bedott."
14. *Richard Harlow*: another female impersonator whose autograph appears in the litho, but no data available on why the numbers "1492" appears. In spite of the outfit, Richard still looks like a linebacker to me.
15. *Captain January*: famous fictional character, Captain January was a lighthouse keeper at Cape Tempest, Maine, who had to raise a small girl whose parents' boat capsized. The story was finally made into a movie with Guy Kibbe playing the Captain and Shirley Temple starring as the little girl. This is undoubtedly one of the best artworks produced by Schlegel Litho.
16. *Sandow*: famous strongman who appeared all over the world.

*1. Lillian Russell *****
*2. William Gillette ****
*3. Ethel Barrymore *****

1.

2.

3.

4. Irish Singer **
5. Rudolph Valentino ***
6. Kyra **
7. Clint Ford **

4.

5.

RUDOLPH
VALENTINO

6.

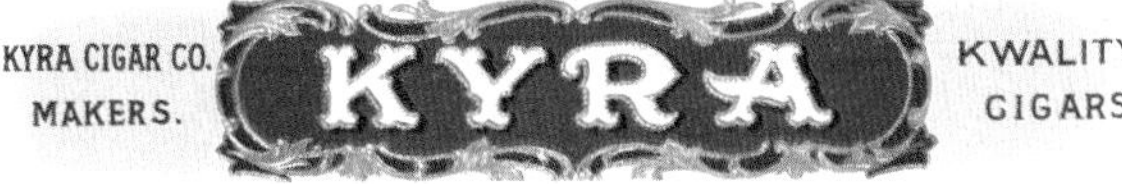

7.

CLINT FORD

*8. Arthur Donaldson ***
*9. Gabler's Judge ***
*10. Lillian Ashley ***
*11. Jean Valjean ***
*12. Three Twins **

8.

9.

11.

10.

12.

THREE TWINS

"A HOWLING SUCCESS"

THREE TWINS

*13. Neil Burgess ****
*14. Richard Harlow ****
*15. Captain January *****
*16. Sandow *****

13.

14.

15.

16.

PATRIOTISM

Since the images on the cigar labels of the Golden Era reflected the passions of those cigar smokers from Sports and Gambling all the way up to Transportation and Women, they also show us that he loved his country. Even before the Spanish-American War, labels portrayed American flags, banners, eagles, Columbia, and Uncle Sam who was created by Thomas Nast. Revolutionary War heroes and Civil War heroes from both sides graced cigar box labels, and with the onset of the Spanish-American War, the lithographic artists came forth with a whole new array of artworks commemorating every general, admiral, naval battle and victory reported in the comparatively short war.

1. *American Glory*: Although the title of this label has been inserted later by letter press, (which means it probably bore a variety of titles) you can see that the American Litho artist even colored Columbia's wings red, white and blue, while inserting a sword, shields, olive branch and stars, not wanting to miss a trick. As an afterthought, he even inserted the heads of Indian chiefs at the bottom!
2. *National Draft*: This artist attempted to give the label credibility with a certificate type border, a guarantee of quality, and an appeal to pride motivator saying they will please "gentlemen" with the most fastidious taste. In an effort to give the impression of federal backing (which was untrue) he added an eagle clutching a Cuban flag and our capitol building.
3. *America's Pride*, *American Citizen* and *Los Inmortales*: George Washington was a favorite subject of label artists, and his image was always portrayed in association with heroism or patriotism.

In *America's Pride*, he is flanked by the slogan "First in War, First in Peace, and First in the Hearts of Countrymen." What impressed me most about this label, over and above being an extremely well done chromolithograph was the fact that the artist, in great detail, added an excellent miniature drawing of Washington crossing the Delaware below his portrait, capturing every minute detail including the embossing of ice chunks floating in the river.

American Citizen: This label (which also appears in its actual form in this book) was created at the turn of the century in an effort to capitalize on the patriotic surge from the Spanish-American War and the protectionist attitude generated to promote American products made by American citizens, initiated by the efforts of former cigar roller and president of the AFL, Samuel Gompers.

Los Inmortales: "The Immortals" created by Louis Wagner of New York but actually printed in Germany featured Washington between two other famous presidents, Abraham Lincoln and Ulysses S. Grant, who had just passed away. Although it was created at the time of Grant's death, Washington still held center stage.

4. After his creation by Thomas Nast on the pages of Harper's Weekly, "Uncle Sam" started appearing in a variety of patriotic themes including cigar labels.

Uncle Sam: One of the earliest non-embossed images of Uncle Sam to grace cigar box labels was created by the Klingenberg Litho of Detmold, Germany. Since they maintained offices around the globe including one in New York, their American branch must have requested that they produce this rendition. This extremely high quality piece of art was printed on the very early grooved paper used in the 1880's and is probably the best quality Uncle Sam label ever found.

Wide-Awake: Jumping on the bandwagon after the Spanish-American War victory, the litho artist depicted "Uncle Sam" with the American Eagle perched on a cannon and powerful U.S. Naval war ship in the background.

Honest Yankee: This label, created by an imaginative American Litho artist shows a "lay-back" Uncle Sam admiring his own cigars with a map of the United States as a background. Although this could never compete with the Klingenberg produced label from an art standpoint, it is a good example of the American Litho Company's creative art staff.

5. The Spanish American War proved to be a bonanza for the lithographers and cigar smoker to share in our nations glory and military strength.

American Cruisers: This sample label produced by Krueger and Braun depicts the pride of the American fleet at full steam ahead either towards Cuba or the Philippines and the Battle of Manila.

Solid Shot: This artist from the George Schlegel Litho Company really tied the war into this cigar brand by having the cannons shoot giant cigars at the enemy!

Rough Riders: There were few heroes more beloved than Col. Teddy Roosevelt during this period, so it was quite logical to depict his famous charge up San Juan Hill on a label. This art was used profusely on posters and signs by a number of advertisers, but was most popular in Tampa, Florida, which Roosevelt used as his port of embarkment for the Cuban assault.

American Conquest: Basking in the glow of our most recent victory, the cigar makers even honored the "peace Commissioners," Senators George Gray, Cushman K. Davis, W.P. Frye and Justice W.R. Day and Whitelaw Reid who negotiated the terms of the Surrender and the Disposition of the Philippines, Puerto Rico and Cuba.

6. Politicians have always used patriotism as a motivator to gain votes, so it was quite natural that the political parties would want to expose their candidates to the cigar smoking voters through this already accepted medium. Although very few survived, cigars and cigar boxes promoting one candidate or another far outnumber political buttons produced during the same period, but the cigars promoting the candidates had an additional unique benefit, they were used to create straw polls. Boxes of cigars promoting both candidates were displayed open in the display case side by side. On a blackboard the results of the preferences of cigar smokers for one candidate or another were then recorded.

Labels: *Cleveland and Stevenson* and *Harrison and Reid* The Schmidt Litho Company of New York offered these examples to cigar makers during their campaigns. You will notice that they are stock labels with black and white photos "dropped in."

7. *Franklin D. Roosevelt*: This brand was probably not created for any campaign or straw poll, but merely an effort on the part of the cigar maker to capitalize on Roosevelt's popularity and sell cigars to Roosevelt followers.

1. *American Glory* ***
2. *National Draft* **
3. *America's Pride* **

1.

2.

National Draft
To Whom It May Concern:
These Cigars are guaranteed to be uniform in quality and appeal to the judgment of every Gentleman. They will please the most fastidious taste.
SELECTIVE
SELECTIVE
· A GENERAL FAVORITE ·

3.

*3. American Citizen ***
*Los Inmortales ****
*4. Uncle Sam ****
*Wide-Awake ***

3.

3.

4.

4.

Honest Yankee **
5. American Cruisers ****
Solid Shot ****
Rough Riders ****
American Conquest ***

4.

5.

5.

5.

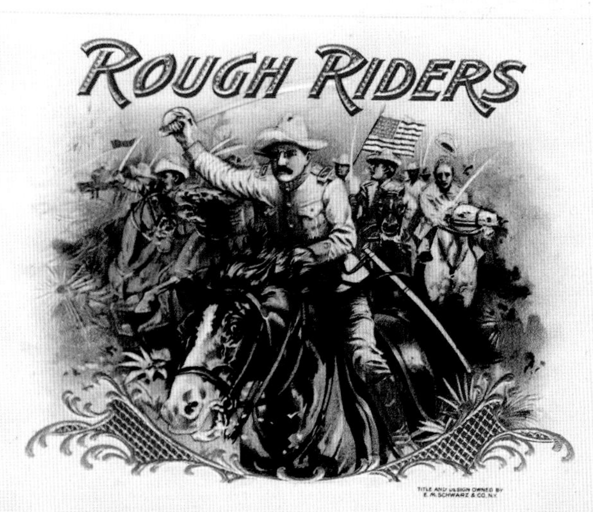

5.

6. Cleveland and Stevenson ****
Harrison and Reid ****
7. Franklin D. Roosevelt **

6.

6.

7.

TRANSPORTATION

lthough transportation is only considered a minor theme among cigar label subjects, they certainly are popular with the collector's of today. Taking into consideration all the progress made during the Industrial Revolution and the Golden Era of the cigar age, it was quite logical that the artists would attempt to enhance their products by featuring many of the new-fangled inventions. Trains, the backbone of our country's dramatic growth spurt and the vehicles that opened up the west were "naturals" as cigar label themes, and appeared as early as the 1860's on cigar boxes and lasted for almost 100 years.

1. One of the earliest train labels was one produced by Heppenheimer and Mauer called *Prairie* giving the smoker the impression that wild game, especially the American bison existed in great numbers, but they were not slaughtered to keep the trains moving, but to rob the American Indians of their main food source which was the master plan of General Sherman. Sherman's plan did not starve the Indians, but in the process almost made the American bison extinct.
2. An extremely popular brand featuring a train was the S. S. Pierce Co. of Boston's *Overland* showing both the early and later versions which the Pierce Company changed as trains became more steamlined. There were actually four versions produced with only a few slight modifications on each, but the last version shown here with two trains shows the oldest and newest side by side.
3. *Covered Wagon*: Although very few people were still using covered wagons when this label was produced, the image of the pioneers was still romanticized in this outstanding piece of art done by Calvert Litho of Detroit.
4. *Aero*: Always ready to promote cigars with any new and miraculous feat, the Geo. Schlegel Litho Co. produced this sample label honoring the first steerable airship which circled the Eiffel Tower twice and sailed against the wind on November 19, 1899.
5. While the Europeans honored Bleriot, the Frenchman who flew from Dover to Calais across the English Channel in 1909, on a cigar label, American Aviation labels were quite scarce until Lindberg crossed the Atlantic in the "Spirit of St. Louis." Here are three versions: *World's Greatest Flyer*,

Spirit of St. Louis and *Our Bird* which were very popular.
6. Not to be outdone by the competition, the J. P. Alley Company put a Negro in their plane and called him *Hambone*. This is an original example of a sign which hung from fans in cigar and drug store ceilings.
7. *Car Line*: Taking advantage of the popularity of another new mode of transportation was the E. H. Chandler Company of Minneapolis who had the Calvert Litho Company create a modern looking street car which supposedly ran from Minneapolis to St. Paul.
8. When it came to nautical themes, the artists again attempted to depict the fastest and most modern ships available and even honored the America's Cup winner with the label called *Cup Defender*.
9. *Clipper*: The harbors of Boston were filled with clipper ships when this label was produced, and was the fastest and most modern for its time.
10. *Whale-Back*: As merchant shipping became more and more modernized the unusual looking Whale-Back tankers caught the attention of the lithographic artists. This particular label is on display in the Nautical section of the Smithsonian Institute and was also featured as an example in Time Life's Encyclopedia of Collectibles.
11. *Road Queens*: When bicycles became more streamlined with inflatable tires, and no large wheel up front, the lithographers were right there to try to affiliate themselves with this new innovation. In this case, they took it a step further, showing the new "modern women" riding them.
12. With the introduction of the automobile, you would assume that the litho artist's would have a field day with the variety of contraptions being introduced. Surprisingly enough, after perusing tobacco leaf journal records, very few labels featuring automobiles were registered during the first two decades of this century. I have seen labels titled *Automobilist* and even Lady *Automobilist* and both appeared to be electric cars.

If you study some of the newspapers and other publications of the period, the general populace had a bit of a problem accepting these "horseless carriages," and many early automobile owners were considered as "kooks" by today's standards. That is one possibility why the cigar makers shunned the auto as a possible marketing tool. Interestingly enough, when the artists developed labels featuring an important looking building like a major cigar factory or the First National Bank, they managed to incorporate a few cars into the street scenes. Using the *First National Bank* label as an example, although the artist included a "modern" car and an electric streetcar in the scene, there was also a horse and buggy in front of the bank during this "transition" period.

But even if cars weren't romantic, speed was. This image of an early racer on what appears to be Daytona Beach was aptly titled *Speed King* in an effort to attract the sports-minded smokers. Even the Chicago Automobile Club in 1922 avoided portraying any particular style of auto and chose a character with Mercury type wings on his hat and a steering wheel in his hands "burning up the road" titled *Motorist*.

1. Prairie ****

1.

Inside—No. 1676—$20.00 per 1000.
Outside—No. 1677—$10.00 per 1000.

2.

2. Overland (early) ***
Overland (later) **
3. Covered Wagon **
4. Aero ****

S. S. PIERCE CO.

4.

S. S. PIERCE

2.

OVERLAND

3.

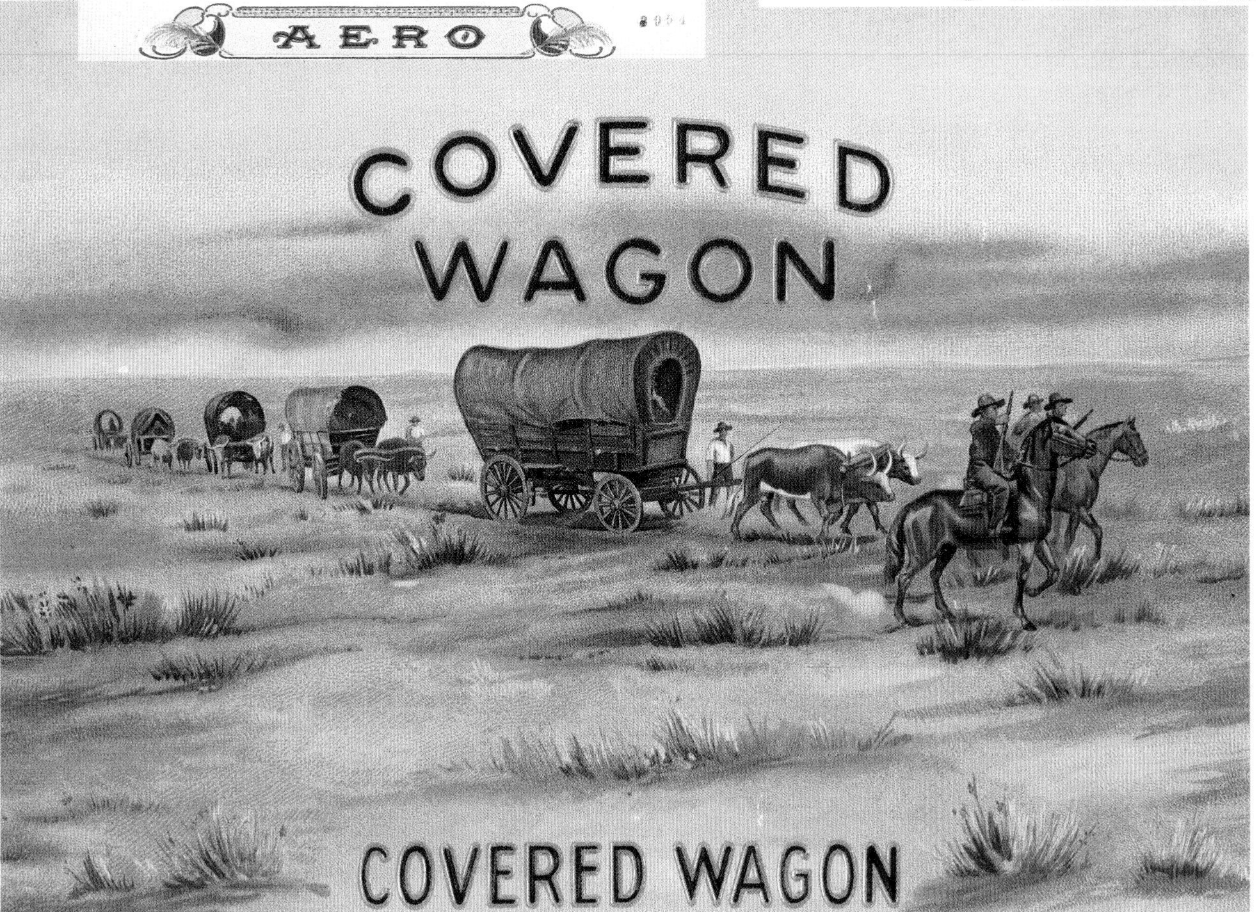

*5. World's Greatest Flyer ****
*Spirit of St. Louis ***
*Our Bird **
*6. Hambone *****
*7. Car Line *****
*8. Cup Defender *****
*9. Clipper ****
*10. Whale-Back ***

WORLD'S FLYER GREATEST

5.

5.

5¢

MAZER-CRESSMAN CIGAR CO. INC. **SPIRIT OF ST. LOUIS** DETROIT, MICH.

J.
HA
5¢
FI
FIN

6.

5.

OUR U S A B

THE LONE EAGLE
GOOD WILL FLY

5¢ OUR BIR

WHALE-BACK

10.

9.

7.

8.

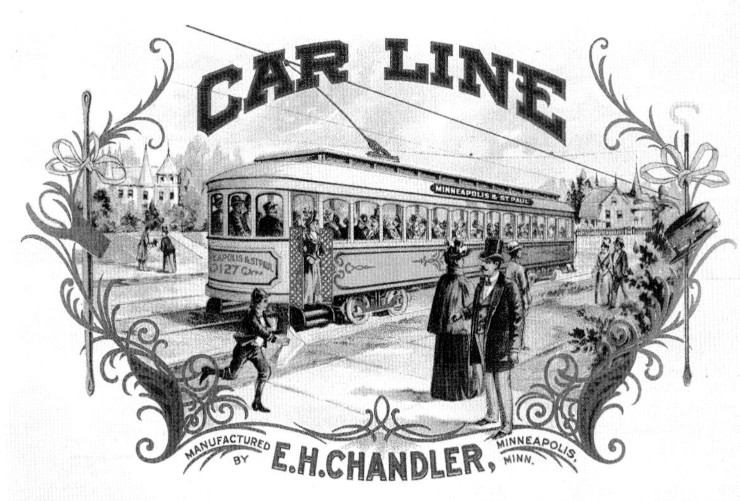

SMOKE CUP DEFENDER CIGARS

*11. Road Queens ****
*12. Speed King *****
*Motorist ***

11.

12.

12.

Sports & Gambling

Sports and gambling were obviously very popular pastimes of the cigar smoking men of the golden era. Interestingly enough, very few of these images have survived and are numerically almost as rare as nudes. We can only guess that some of these subjects were frowned upon by the masses and that, like the brands featuring nudes and scarlet women, sports and gambling brands were limited to the clubs and other outlets frequented by men only. Those few examples that have survived are considered quite rare and valuable and have fallen into the "cross-collectibles" category since baseball, tennis, boxing and gambling collectors have historically outbid cigar label collectors for images picturing their favorite sport.

1. *Club Friends*: produced by Schmidt Litho features a friendly and relaxing game of pool while smoking cigars. In an effort to "upgrade" the image of the sport the artist dressed them in tuxedos.
2. *First Round*: created by Heppenheimer and Sons was certainly more of a "saloon type" brand, and since this is a sample, we can't be sure it was ever produced.
3. *Golf Links*: an unusual and outstanding piece of art by the Louis E. Nueman Co. of New York, showing men and women playing golf together but I'm sure that most of the general populace could never identify with this scene.
4. *Crack Team*: another great piece of art by Louis E. Nueman showing a sandlot baseball game.
5. *Crack Runner*: anything great must have been "crack." In the 1800's this very early racing scene, also by Nueman was a very typical horse racing scene before the lithographers started doing portraits of well-known race horses.
6. *Hans Wagner*: a very controversial label produced by the Geo. Schlegel Litho Company for the Freeman Cigar Company tried to get around Honus Wagner's refusal to promote tobacco products or alcohol by calling it the "Hans" Wagner brand. Wagner did stop the Sweet Caporal Cigarette Cards, and supposedly 38 of them survived to end up in private collections. I believe the cigar label is actually rarer since I can personally document only 18 survivors.
7. *Ursus*: now here's a sport! The gladiator in the coliseum is wrestling a bull with a naked beauty

tied to its horns under moonlight and torches! This blockbuster image was created by the Calvert Litho Co. of Detroit.

8. *National Sportsman*: early 1900's label produced when Teddy Roosevelt was promoting the pleasures and benefits of the outdoors.

9. *Northeastern Michigan Booster*: Michigan, a state that even today, heavily promotes their outdoor activities, saw one of their own regional Chamber of Commerce Booster Clubs produce a cigar for their visitors.

10. *Sea Robin*: the W. B. Lenz Company of Brooklyn, New York, had Schlegel Litho produce this unusual brand that I assume was to be sold along the seashore, but I honestly can't identify the fish that the artist created. Considering the amount of time that has passed, they're probably another species that has appeared on cigar labels but is now extinct!

11. *Straight Five*: the O.L. Schwencke Company tied the theme of a straight flush–a poker player's dream to the fact that all cigars were 5¢.

12. *Grand Ouvert*: this was just another theme using the "perfect hand" in the game of skat to compare with the Otto Berndt Cigar brand.

13. *Hey-Yea Get A Lead*: this two color label of famous player Hughie Jennings was probably produced by F. M. Howell. Only 110 are known to exist in varying conditions, but have consistently set new price levels since their discovery in 1987. Prices have stayed in the $400 to $500 range, and probably were grabbed up initially by baseball collectors (another cross-collectible), but a beautifully framed example, including an actual photo of Hughie Jennings, did reach $1,000 at a fund-raiser in Ohio recently.

Hughie Jennings is a Hall of Famer, former All-Star short stop for Baltimore and manager of the Detroit Tigers winning two American League pennants (having Ty Cobb on his team didn't hurt). "Hey-Yea" or "EEE-Yah" "Get a Lead" was what Jennings used to shout at his base runners. The labels were discovered by dealer Leonard Lasko.

14. *Frontier*: produced by the Nave-McCord Mercantile Company in St. Joseph, Missouri. This image was used on every product they distributed from cigars to spinach.

*1. Club Friends *****

1.

2. *First Round* ****
3. *Golf Links* ****
4. *Crack Team* ****

2.

Inside No.—2882 $25.00 per 1000.
Outside No.—2883—$15.00 per 1000.

3.

DESIGN OWNED BY L. E. NEUMAN & CO.
LOUIS E. NEUMAN & CO. | No. 1259-Ins. $ 1.70 per 100 NET.
N. W. Cor. Pearl & Elm Streets, New York | „ 1260-Outs. $ 0.80 per 100 NET.
Special Prices in lots of 1000. ALSO BLANKS.

4.

TITLE & DESIGN OWNED BY L. E. NEUMAN & CO.

LOUIS E. NEUMAN & CO.,
N. W. Cor. Pearl & Elm Streets, New York.

No. 1308—INS., $1 70 per 100. Net.
No. 1309—OUTS, $0.80 per 100. Net.

ALSO BLANKS.
Special Prices in lots of 1000.

SMOKE CRACK TEAM CIGAR

5. Crack Runner ****
6. Hans Wagner ****
7. Ursus ****
8. National Sportsman **
9. Northeastern Michigan Booster **

8.

NATIONAL SPORTSMAN

9.

5.

THE CRACK RUNNER

WESTERN BRANCH,
Nº 7 S. CLARK ST.
CHICAGO, ILL.

LOUIS E. NEUMAN & CO.,
N. W. Cor. Pearl & Elm Streets, New York.
No. 1112–Ins.–$25.00 per 1000, $2.75 per 100.
" 1113–Outs–$19.00 " " $1.10. "
ALSO BLANKS.

6.

7.

*10. Sea Robin ***
*11. Straight Five ****

10.

11.

12. Grand Ouvert ***
13. Hey-Yea Get A Lead ****
14. Frontier ****

12.

13.

BY PERMISSION *Hughie Jennings*

5c CIGAR 5c

14.

FRONTIER
1846

NAVE-McCORD MERCANTILE Co.

HOUSE & PRIVATE BRANDS

From the very beginning of merchandising cigars in boxes, independent merchants, restaurants, tobacconists, men's clubs, banks and athletic clubs began ordering cigars labeled exclusively for their company, and have been popular ever since. Just as Sears & Roebuck used outside manufacturers to produce their house brands of appliances, sporting goods, tools and automotive products (they also sold private brand cigars and canned goods before World War II) merchants wanted their name prominently displayed on the boxes.

Although many were created for places where cigars were sold, many large corporations and individuals had brands created to be given away as executive gifts. Don't be confused by such brands as *Yellow Cab*, *Canadian Club*, *Sunmaid*, or *Old Dutch* since "name borrowing" was common among cigar manufacturers.

The ultimate example of a private brand which could also be considered a vanity label was the recent discovery at auction of a box of cigars complete with family crest on the label of Reich Marshall Herman Goering which sold for $1,800 at auction.

*1. Bohemian Club of San Francisco ****
*2. Bullocks Dept. Store **
*3. Cleveland Athletic Club ***
*4. Dime Bank of Detroit ***
*5. Harvard Club of New York City **

1.

2.

3.

4.

*6. Illinois Auto Club**
*7. Los Angeles Country Club**
*8. Milwaukee Athletic Club****
*9. St. Francis Club**

BY PERMISSION OF ILLINOIS AUTOMOBILE CLUB

7.

8.

Under personal supervision of Pancho Arango

MILWAUKEE ATHLETIC CLUB

9.

5.

10. Tampa Speedway •
11. Union Pacific Railroad •
12. University Club of Chicago •
13. University Club of New York •

10.

MANUFACTURED EXCLUSIVELY FOR R. S. BARFIELD, BOX 5311, JACKSONVILLE, FLA.

11.

Made Exclusively For
THE UNION PACIFIC RAILROAD
By The
Morgan Cigar Co. Inc., Tampa, Fla.

13.

12.

FAMOUS MEN

ost cigar industry historians have to agree that although a major thrust to motivate the men who bought cigars was to depict scenes of things that men liked–i.e., sports, leisure, women, gambling, patriotism, etc.–the all-time winner in pure numbers has to be famous men. It is not completely apparent that the cigar makers and lithographers recognized this trend right away, but once they did, they dug through every history book and newspaper to choose some type of hero that the smoker might identify with.

Here are just a small percentage of the famous men that actually made it to the cigar box.

1. *Barrister*: Benjamin Disraeli, attorney, statesman, and Prime Minister of England.
2. *Captain Sam Brady*: famous Indian fighter after whom Brady Lake and Brady's Leap were named. Brady's Leap is a point in the Cuyahoga River in Kent, Ohio where Brady supposedly leaped across after escaping from his Indian captors. Brady Lake is supposedly where he hid from them under water while breathing through a reed.
3. *Cervantes*: the famous writer.
4. *John Carver*: first governor of Plymouth Colony in 1620.
5. *Champ Clark*: famous politician of Missouri.
6. *Charles the Great*: Charlemagne, Frankish King, Emperor of the West. Legend enhanced and distorted his actual achievements and he became the central figure of a medieval romance cycle.
7. *Henry Clews*: famous financier.
8. *Commander*: picturing General "Black Jack" Pershing.
9. *Colonial Orator*: Patrick Henry.
10. *Commoner*: a man of the people, Oliver Cromwell, English religious zealot and leader.
11. *Dante*: famous author; this is the earliest version created by George Schlegel Litho for the Sulzberger-Oppenheimer Company and is an extremely coveted label because of its great art.
12. *Da Vinci:* the supreme example of Renaissance genius, as painter, sculptor, architect, musician, engineer and scientist.

13. *Erin's Pride*: poet and author, Robert Emmet.
14. *Farragut*: Civil War Admiral famous for the Battle of New Orleans.
15. *Fellow Citizens*: outstanding rendition of Generals Grant and Lee created by Calvert Litho of Detroit; extremely rare.
16. *Gallatin*: Albert Gallatin, Secretary of the Treasury 1801-1813.
17. *General Custer*: one of the earliest renditions of Custer on a cigar label for the Auer Cigar Company of Syracuse, New York; extremely rare.
18. *Gettysburg Commanders*: outstanding label by Globe Litho of New York honoring Generals Hancock, Meade and Reynolds.
19. *Edmund Halley*: created by Consolidated Litho for the Ben Kane Company of Philadelphia to honor the famous astronomer after the 1910 comet sighting.
20. *General Hartranft*: famous Civil War general.
21. *Hoosier Poet*: honoring James Whitcomb Riley. Riley appeared on three other labels with different titles.
22. *Jack Necker*: famous sportsman.
23. *Joe Cannon*: famous Republican Speaker of the House.
24. *National Speaker*: another version honoring Joe Cannon.
25. *John, Sr.*: polished gentleman in tuxedo rumored to be John Barrymore, Sr.
26. *Judge Wright*: very famous brand created by the M & N Cigar Company of Cleveland, Ohio.
27. *Judge Ross*: unknown judge who gave his permission to use his image.
28. *King Alfred*: medieval English king.
29. *LaRochelle*: another great piece of art created by Calvert Litho honoring Cardinal Richilieu who defeated the Huegonots at La Rochelle, France.
30. *Lincoln Bouquet*: Lincoln was a very popular subject in the North.
31. *Little Tom*: Thomas Morton, famous politician.
32. *Henry W. Longfellow*: famous writer shown.
33. *Francis Marbois*: Finance Minister to Napoleon who negotiated the Louisiana Purchase.
34. *Mark Twain*: great label produced by the Wolf Brothers Cigar Company at the time of his death in 1910.
35. *Marshall Foch*: French World War I leader.
36. *Monroe Doctrine*: created for the W. F. Monroe Cigar Company in Chicago, who were looking to capitalize on some possible ties with our fifth president.
37. *J. Sterling Morton*: created for the Saeger & Sons Cigar Company of Fremont, Nebraska. Morton was a Nebraska politician who is best known for his creation of Arbor Day.
38. *Old Hickory*: unique rendition honoring Andrew Jackson.
39. *General Wm. J. Palmer*: pioneer of the Colorado railroad, vignettes show steam engine and the Antlers resort which he founded.
40. *Pinzon*: Martin Pinzon commander of the Pinta, one of Christopher Columbus' three vessels on his first voyage to the New World, is the man who suggested on Oct. 7, 1492 that they change course which brought their first sight of land in the Bahamas on Oct. 12. Created for the Van Dam Cigar Company of Grand Rapids, Michigan by Schlegel Litho.
41. *Professor Morse*: created for the Cuban Cigar Company of Cleveland (which only lasted one year) by Consolidated Litho. The label features both Samuel F.B. and his brother Sidney. Although Samuel is best known by the masses for his invention of Morse Code, he was a very famous painter and sculptor. He founded and became first president of the National Academy of Design in New York, and established the department of Fine Arts at New York University. One of his paintings "The Gallery of the Louvre" was recently purchased for 3.25 million dollars by Daniel J. Terra, President Reagan's Ambassador at-large for Cultural Affairs. His brother Sidney, founded the New York newspaper, the "Observer", and was an inventor in his own right, inventing a method of making stereotype plates from wax and a bathometer for exploring the depths of the sea.
42. *Pulaski:* famous Polish General who served under George Washington in the Revolutionary War.
43. *Charles M. Russell*: famous western artist who also created a few works for cigar labels.
44. *Walter Scott*: famous Scottish novelist and poet. In 1813, he assumed responsibility for Ballantyne's, a printing firm, paying its expenses from Scott's advances from his publishers. After a depression in 1825 ruined both companies, he declared bankruptcy. Scott set out to pay all debts, but it destroyed his health. After his death, the debts were met by the earnings of his books.
45. *Shakespeare*: popular brand created by the famous Sanchez and Haya Factory #1 in Tampa.

46. *Socrates*: famous Greek philosopher; great art done by Schlegel Litho.
47. *Silver Prince*: supposed rendition of Moses by Heywood-Strasser-Voigt Litho of New York.
48. *Sunset Club*: a private club on the banks of Lake Michigan. The label features the famous magnates: Pullman, Leiter, Gage, Armour, Rockefeller and Carnegie.
49. *Ben Tracy*: American general, lawyer and secretary of the navy.
50. *Daniel Boone*: famous pioneer.

*1. Barrister ****
*2. Captain Sam Brady ***
*3. Cervantes ***
*4. John Carver **

1.

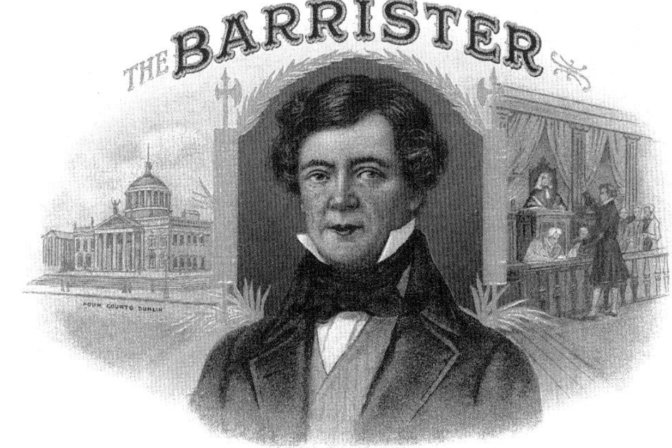

3.

2.

4.

*5. Champ Clark **
*6. Charles the Great **
*7. Henry Clews ***
*8. Commander **
*9. Colonial Orator **
*10. Commoner ***

5.

STAR THOMPSON TOBACCO CO. **CHAMP CLARK** TAMPA FLA.

COMMO

6.

8.

5¢ Commander 5¢

7.

HENRY CLEWS

9.

*11. Dante *****
*12. Da Vinci ****
*13. Erin's Pride ***
*14. Farragut ***
*15. Fellow Citizens *****

10.

11.

13.

15.

14.

16. *Gallatin* **
17. *General Custer* ***
18. *Gettysburg Commanders* ***
19. *Edmund Halley* **
20. *General Hartranft* **

16.

17.

19.

18.

20.

21. Hoosier Poet **
22. Jack Necker ***
23. Joe Cannon **
24. National Speaker *

JOE CANNON

23.

22.

24.

VERY MILD — SPECIAL SELECTION

NATIONAL SPEAKER

21.

HOOSIER POET

*25. John, Sr. ***
*26. Judge Wright **
*27. Judge Ross **
*28. King Alfred ***
*29. LaRochelle ***
*30. Lincoln Bouquet ****

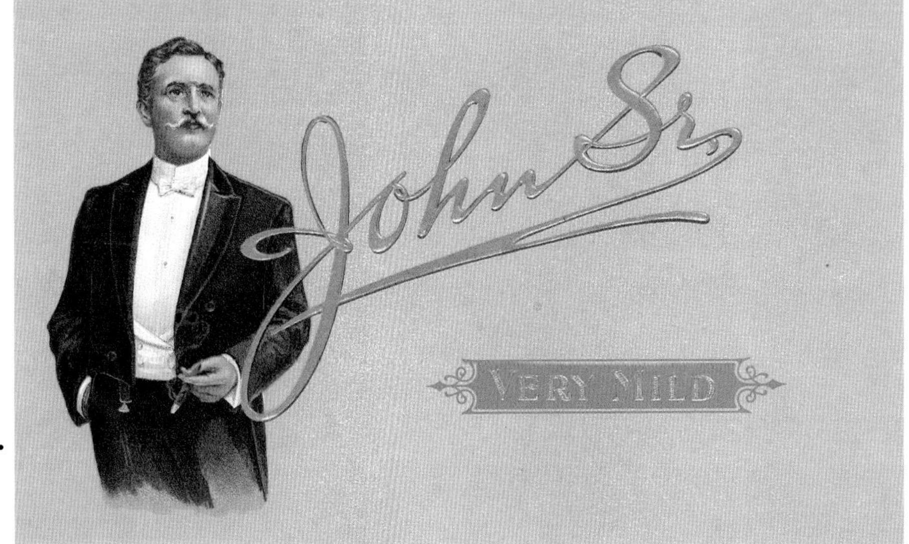

25.

26.

2 for 15¢

Made in Tampa

A FAIR TRIAL WILL GIVE A VERDICT IN FAVOR OF THIS CIGAR

JUDGE WRIGHT

28.

27. 2 for 5¢

JUDGE ROSS

BY PERMISSION.

Low In Price But High In Quality

JUDGE ROSS

30.

29.

31.

31. Little Tom **
32. Henry W. Longfellow ***
33. Francis Marbois **
34. Mark Twain **
35. Marshall Foch **

33.

32.

34.

MARK TWAIN

MARSHAL FOCH

35.

36. Monroe Doctrine **
37. J. Sterling Morton **
38. Old Hickory **
39. General Wm. J. Palmer **
40. Pinzon *
41. Professor Morse *

36.

40.

37.

W.F. MONROE CIGAR CO. MONROE DOCTRINE CHICAGO ILLINOIS

39.

GEN. WM J. PALMER

38.

41.

CUBAN CIGAR CO. PROFESSOR MORSE CLEVELAND, OHIO.

42. Pulaski **
43. Charles M. Russell ****
44. Walter Scott ***
45. Shakespeare ***

43.

44.

42.

45.

*46. Socrates ***
*47. Silver Prince ***
*48. Sunset Club ****
*49. Ben Tracy ***
*50. Daniel Boone *****

47.

46.

48.

50.

49.

FAMOUS WOMEN

From very early on, the creative staffs of the lithographic companies in cooperation with the cigar makers, realized that with a clientele that was over 90% men, they should create images of things men liked. Once you have perused through thousands of subjects created by these artists, you can most certainly see that famous men, sports, animals and exotic places were popular themes, but men's hormonal balances were not much different 100 years ago, and it is quite obvious from the labels pictured throughout this book that men certainly liked women!

Women of all ages, walks of life and stages of dress and undress appeared on labels, and in an effort to possibly motivate the women's libbers of the 19th century, some women even appeared in mannish type dress. Although some labels pictured women bare-breasted and in various stages of undress which were quite risque for the 19th Century, these brands were usually relegated to the private men's clubs and poolrooms and hardly ever appeared in drugstores or retailers dealing with the general public.

The cigar makers realized that although the 19th Century men had normally active hormones and liked to sow a few wild oats, the woman he wants to marry must be pure, chaste and rather demure, which is why the lion's share of labels produced showed sweet and smiling maidens with a romantic gaze. The labels pictured in this section run the complete gamut from semi-nudes and suggestive to chaste maidens and liberated women.

1. The *Speckled Sumatra* label showing a slightly rubinesque lady half draped with a blanket and jewels was probably quite popular in private clubs. This label has also surfaced with the title *Full Dress* and *Good Shape* although the diet faddists of today might disagree about her shape.

2. *Belle Peep* is one of those tongue in cheek productions by the creative staff of American Litho in 1902 saying she was "the best in the field."
3. *Florida Widow* is another slightly titillating subject since widows and divorcees were considered fair game for the "dudes" and "swells" of the 19th Century.
4. *Wedding Veil* produced by Charles Boak of Harrisburg, Pa. snaps the young dudes back into reality reminding them that marriage is the only way to go.
5. *Bessie Green* (also sold as *Ruby Lips*), *La Meloda, Signal Perfecto, La Mareva, Lady Mary, Pearl, Sweet Belle* and *City Pride* give us an outstanding insight into the fashion of the times.
6. Women of varying degrees of fame also graced cigar labels, with *Betsy Ross, Marie Antoinette* and *Martha Washington* being reasonably identifiable.

Whether *Irish Beauty Lady Kildare* ever made it to the cigar box is not known, but *Peggy O'Neal,* unkindly nick-named "Pot-house Peggie" by the press, was long a subject of controversy.

A tavern girl, she married John Eaton, Jackson's Secretary of War. The vignette on the left shows her being accepted at a dinner by President Jackson with all the other cabinet wives fuming and storming out of the dinner. The vignette on the right shows her husband, John Eaton, in a duel over an insult to her honor. Eaton resigned from Jackson's cabinet in 1834 and became governor of Florida. This brand survived for quite a while, and proves that Americans liked the underdog even 100 years ago!

American Belle, Moonbeams, Prima Lucia, Mi Lola, La Rita, Miss Primrose, Sonada, Admiration, Little Quaker even *Sanitary Maid* were very popular brands that pictured the maidens as pure, chaste and even sanitary!

Nebraska Girl, a super piece created by Schmidt Litho for Saeger and Company in Fremont, Nebraska, is an outstanding piece of art.

Madame Butterfly, created by Schlegel Litho was another popular brand that used a spectacular mix of colors.

Lyra and *Madrigal* showed ladies with harps, but the *Lyra* image produced by Calvert Litho was much earlier than *Madrigal* and far superior in artwork.

Famous artists Howard Chandler Christy was given recognition when Geo. Schlegel Litho produced the famous *Christy Girl* brand. Christy was an outstanding artist of women and even did the women for Lucky Strike cigarettes in the 1920s.

Infanta, Calsetta and *Susette* were very imperial in demeanor, while *Madie* has a peasant look.

The *Sun Maid* and *Dutch Maid* labels are proof positive that the cigar makers were not above stealing themes from other products. I could not find any documentation that Sun Maid Raisins or Dutch Maid Cleanser ever caught up with them, but they certainly outlasted them.

In an effort to give women a more liberated appearance the O.L. Schwenke Litho firm created *Our Latest* showing women smoking cigars, and riding the newest design of bicycles in the latest sporty dress.

Schmidt and Company created *Lady Speed* showing a pretty girl driving a speed boat, and Calvert Litho produced *Texie,* a turn-of-the-century female bodybuilder and athlete for the Sutton-Patterson Cigar Co. of Louisville, Kentucky.

I must admit that I was not a big fan of labels depicting women in my early days of collecting, but now realize that many of them are not only outstanding artworks, but an outstanding history lesson.

1. *Speckled Sumatra* **
2. *Belle Peep* ***
3. *Florida Widow* ***

1.

2.

3.

4. Wedding Veil **
5. Bessie Green ****
La Meloda **
Signal Perfecto **

5.

5.

5.

La Mareva *
Lady Mary **
Pearl **

5.

5.

5.

Sweet Belle ***
City Pride ***
6. *Betsy Ross* **
Marie Antionette **

5.

5.

6.

BETSY ROSS

6.

6. *Martha Washington* **
Irish Beauty ***
Peggy O'Neal **
American Belle **

6.

6.

6.

Moonbeams **
Prima Lucia **
Mi Lola **
La Rita **

6.

6.

6.

6.

5¢

6.

Miss Primrose **
Sonada **
Admiration **
Little Quaker **

6.

SONADA

6.

6.

Sanitary Maid **
Nebraska Girl ***
Madame Butterfly ***
Lyra **

6.

6.

6.

6.

6.

Madrigal **
Christy Girl **
Infanta **

6.

6.

Calsetta **
Susette **
Sun Maid **
Dutch Maid **

6.

6.

6.

6.

6.

Our Latest ***
Lady Speed ****
Texie ****

6.

6.

Snap Shot **
Wheeling Maids **
Madie **

6.

SNAP SHOT

6.

ALLAN H. WRIGHT
BELMONT, OHIO.

6.

Children

Although children appeared in all types of early advertising from Runkles Chocolate to Pears Soap, the percentage of cigar brands using children as a theme was rather miniscule compared to all the others. In fact, there were probably more racist themes than ones using children during the golden age. A few exceptions are the *Sonny Boy* pictured here, produced in York, Pennsylvania, which had a long life span, *Sweet Moments* made by C. J. Donovan in Buffalo, New York, did well and Joe Michls *Fifty Little Orphans* was very popular in Indiana. The H. B. Grauley Company in Pennsylvania must have had some success with children since they owned the rights to both *Elsie* and *Our Card*.

No one will ever know how successful *Little Edmund* was, but it appears to be a vanity label from a stock item produced by American Litho. The name *Little Edmund* was letterpressed in at the top, but that's a real photo of a toddler smoking a cigar!

I have no concrete history on the other images as to their success, but I am sure that they were not very motivating factors in helping the cigar smoker choose those brands. In today's art market children's prints sell very well, and with the obviously small percentage of cigar labels produced with children on them, I would definitely consider them a good investment.

1. *50 Little Orphans* ••
2. *Ambition* •••
3. *Blue Poll* •••
4. *Claro-Maduro* ••••
5. *Edna* •••

1.

2.

3.

4.

CLARO-MADURO
NON PLUS ULTRA
REG. U. S. PAT. OFF.

5.

E POLL
E POLL
Manufacturer

EDNA
Smoke EDNA Cigars

6. Elsie **
7. High Toned ***
8. Illinois Club House **

SMOKE ELSIE CIGARS

7.

8.

9. Infantes ••
10. La Tonelda ••

9.

10.

11. Little Edmund •••
12. Little Susie •••

12.

11.

13. Lucky Bill **
14. Memphis Appeal ****

13.

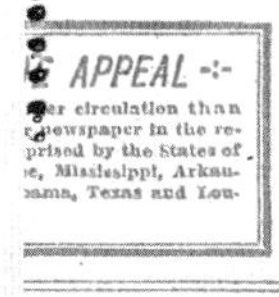

14.

*15. Our Card***
*16. Quaker Boy***
*17. Quality Boy***

15.

OUR CARD

16.

17.

18. Red Dandies ***
19. Sonny Boy **

18.

19.

20. Sweet Moments •••
21. Vega 17 ••

20.

21.

COWBOYS & INDIANS

Cowboys and Indians have always played an important role in American History, so it is quite logical that all the mystery, adventure and romanticism attached to these characters would obviously help sell a variety of consumer products. The cigar makers were no exception, and although we certainly know that many lithographic artists deviated dramatically from historic accuracy in depicting many of their subjects, the images were how they assumed the smokers wanted to visualize the characters. It is very interesting that while the artists were depicting the Negroes, Chinese and Irish as idiots and buffoons, the Red Man was almost always shown as a noble warrior.

Keep in mind that this was a time period when we were still having skirmishes with the Indians from the Dakotas to Arizona, and although the general public never really knew what our government was doing to them, the artist's somehow felt a need to honor and respect them.

Chief Joseph, Red Cloud, Captain Jack, and *Blawk Hawk* were vey real and important historical figures. Although I am sure that the famous *Captain Jack* who was from California never dressed like a Plains Indian. *Indian Corn* makes no sense to me as far as promoting cigars, and *Uwanta* and *Cheekawgo* are typical of the play on words that American Litho creators used at the turn of the century.

Among the cowboy themes, *Pony Post* is a reasonably rare and coveted label and *Dick Custer* who "holds you up" is a humorous, fictional character created by Schlegel Litho. The *Round-Up* label where the cowboy is visualizing himself holding his girlfriend in the campfire smoke quickly replaced the earlier version with no vision and survived for decades. The *Cowboy Hits the Mark* label also created by Schlegel Litho is an outstanding piece of realistic art and you swear that he is aiming straight at you!

When compared to the broad spectrum of subjects used for cigar label art, Cowboys and Indians are quite rare and fast disappearing from the market, so I would strongly advise you not to pass on any that may be offered to you.

1. Abaco ***
2. Best Smoke ***

1.

2.

3. Black Hawk ***
4. Captain Jack ****
5. Chief Joseph ***

4.

5.

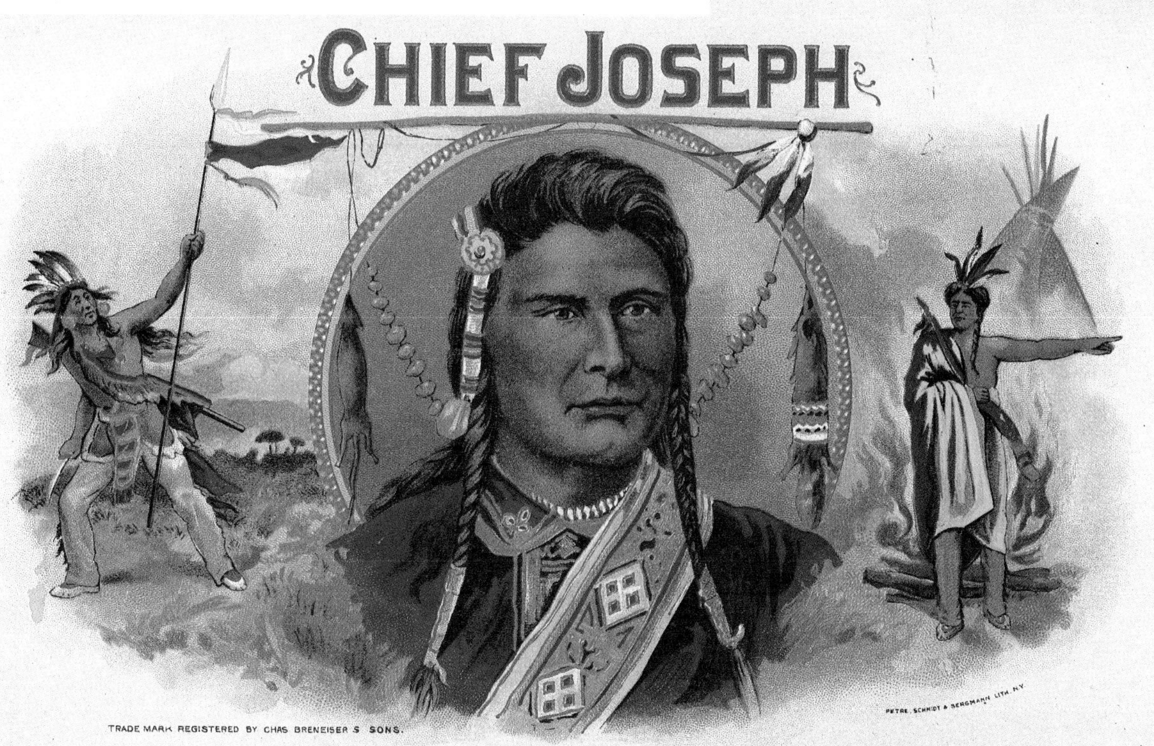

*6. Cowboy Hits the Mark *****
*7. Dick Custer ***

6.

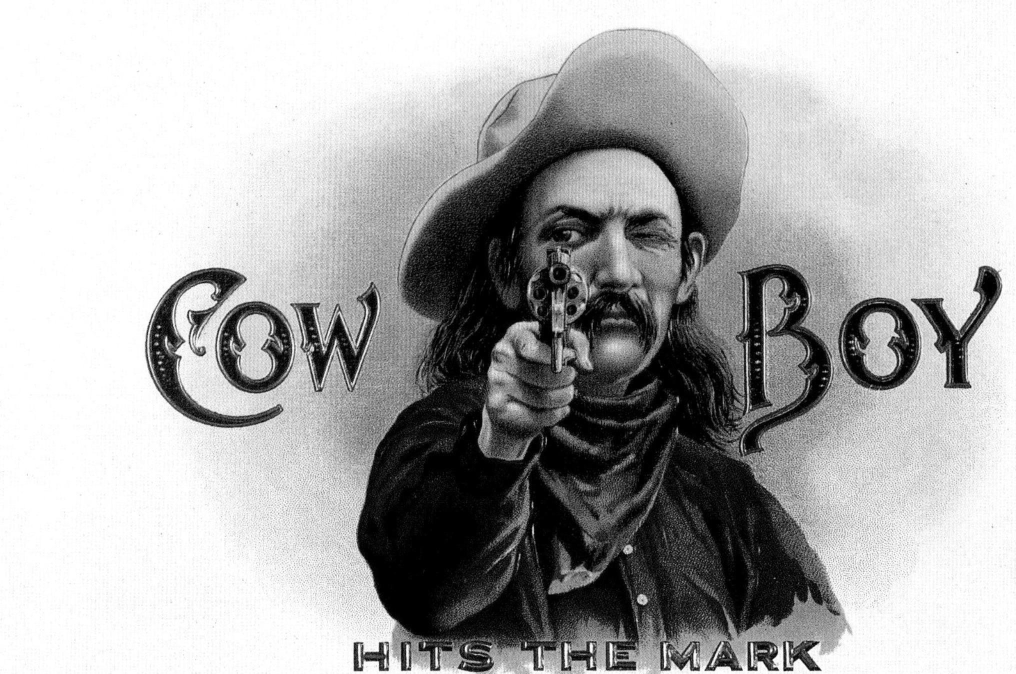

COW BOY
HITS THE MARK
COW BOY

7.

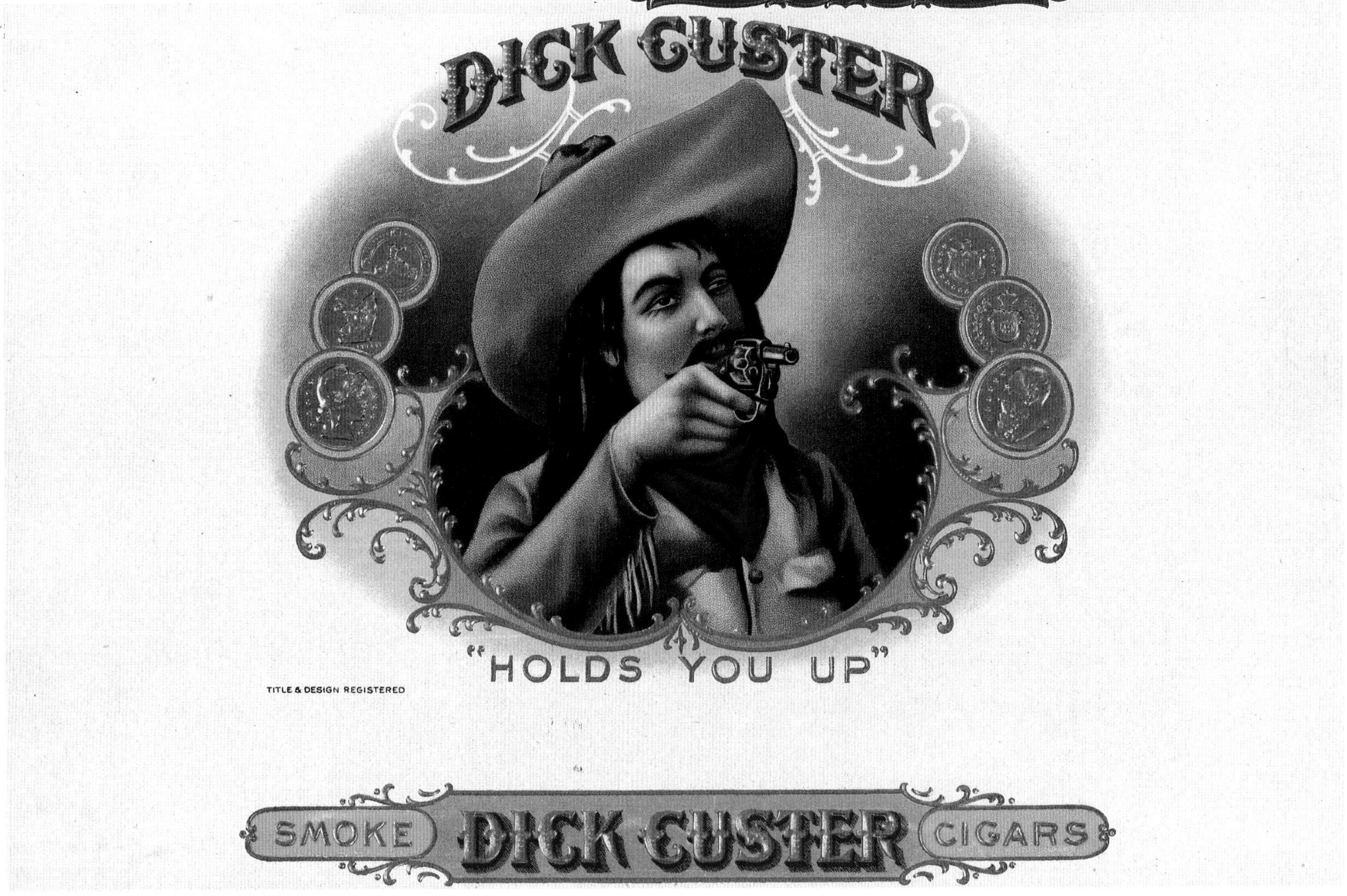
DICK CUSTER
"HOLDS YOU UP"
TITLE & DESIGN REGISTERED
SMOKE DICK CUSTER CIGARS

8. Indian Corn ****
9. Mohawk ***
10. Peace Offering ***

8.

INDIAN CORN

9.

MOHAWK

Joe Reinstein, Maker, WEST POINT, IOWA

10.

11. Pony Post ***
12. Red Cloud ***

11.

12.

*13. Round-Up (alone) ***
*14. Round-Up (with girl) ***
*15. Seminola ***

13.

15.

14.

16. Susquehanna **
17. Uwanta ****
18. Cheekawgo ***

17.

16.

18.

CHEEKAWGO

Blacks

Compared to other theme choices for cigar label art, Blacks are undoubtedly among the rarest. Although blacks were pictured in comical situations and cartoon form to some degree in all 19th and early 20th Century advertising from trade cards up to posters, evidently black subjects were not very effective in selling cigars. For those of you familiar with Black ephemera, blacks were pictured frequently and effectively in marketing household cleaning products, food products and preparations, and performing agricultural chores.

Publications like *Harper's Weekly, Puck, Judge, Leslie's* and many others published between the 1860's-1890's were less kind, printing cartoons of negroes like the "Johnsing Family" and the famous "Blackville" series depicting negroes stealing, fighting, drinking, and getting into a variety of outrageous situations.

Interestingly enough, in the very same time period, there were far more cartoons, ads and editorials attacking and humiliating the Jews, Chinese, and Irish than Blacks. On a basis of pure "tonnage" of negative publicity produced, the attacks on the Irish far outweigh any other ethnic group.

The labels pictured here are a few that did make it to the boxes and had some degree of popularity. *Lime Kiln Club* was one of the earliest published in 1883 and *Little African* survived for many years, produced by the Grauley Company. Some other interesting black titles not pictured include *Nigger Head, Little Alabama Coons, Coon Skin, Ma Honey, and Mixed Pickles.*

1. Lime Kiln Club ****
2. Little Niggers ****

1.

FICE MAY 22nd 1883
B

LITTLE NIGGERS
TICKLED TO DEATH
GUARANTEED HAND MADE LONG HAVANA FILLER SUMATRA WRAPPER

2.

*3. Non-titled negro child picking cotton *****
*4. Little African ****

3.

4.

ANIMALS

nimals were never a major theme before the 1900's, other than the occasional dog or cat at the subjects side, a horse racing scene to motivate the sportsminded smoker, or possibly a subject riding on a horse which was the primary mode of transportation at that time. All that began to change after the 1900's, most likely because the large staffs of artists at such companies as American Litho, O.L. Schwencke, and Schlegel Litho were really pressed for new subject matter, and with the introduction of a few animals and birds into the sample line, they started to catch on.

Race horses were a natural transition, since racing scenes had been depicted in the past, but now the lithographers began to produce portraits of *real* race horses that the smokers possibly were aware of, and by the 1920's any horse that had ever won a major race or set a new record appeared on a cigar label. Pretty soon predatory animals like eagles, lions, tigers and wolves began appearing on labels and were accepted. Cock fighting, an accepted sport of the time, appeared on a number of labels, followed by dogs, cats, birds, fish and even a black bat! Although they could never be categorized as one of the major cigar themes, their comparitive rarity and outstanding artwork make them very much in demand by today's collectors.

1. *Alcazar* and *Peter Manning:* typical race horse labels showing record times, sires and breeders. *Red Tips:* popular "horsey" theme created by Consolidated Litho.
2. *Airedale, Montana Sport* (English Springer Spaniel), *Pug,* and *El Gaurdo* (English Bulldog) showing popular breeds of the time.
3. *Two Friends:* here is a label showing a woman with the popular St. Bernard. Interestingly enough, the brand survived so long that the artists had to change the woman from Victorian dress up to the Flapper style.

4. *Frazzle:* fighting cocks; a very popular brand created by American Litho.
5. *Elkmont* and *Double Elk:* two popular brands produced by Blaine and Annabelle Stewart for the Swisher Cigar Companies.
6. *Crane's Imported:* popular Indiana Company that lasted for decades.
7. *Lone Wolf* and *Big Wolf: Lone Wolf* was created by the Cole Litho Co. of Chicago in 1898, and the extremely lifelike and heavily embossed. *Big Wolf* was created by the Henderson Litho Company of Cincinnati in 1902.
8. *Pig Tail:* one of only a few that featured pigs.
9. *Two Homers:* a sad reminder that the popular homing pigeon of those times is now extinct.
10. *Our Kitties, White Cat* (reclining) and *White Cat* (Puss-In-Boots style): an important household pet of the times, many scenes depicted kittens playing, but one of the *White Cat* producers opted for a cartoonish quality. The *Our Kitties* label with a wood-grain background is superior artwork.
11. *Camel:* no affiliation with the Camel Cigarette people, but an attempt at creating an Egyptian theme which was quite popular in cigarettes.
12. *Two Wheelers:* good art featuring a child with burros.
13. *The Eagle* and *Rex Aguilla* (King of the eagles): semi-patriotic, but featuring our national bird.
14. *Henrietta:* this label was produced to honor the very popular ostrich from the Philadelphia Zoo.
15. *Yellow Hornet* and *Buzzer:* insects even got into the picture by the 1920's, with the imaginative artist turning the butterfly's body into a cigar.
16. *Jersey* and *Hook'em Cow:* Charles Sether of Decatur, Indiana showed the unlikely combination of a Jersey cow with a Spanish Dancer in a tropical setting. Even stranger was the choice of Banneman and List Makers of St. Paul, Minn. who created this image for the South St. Paul, Club. Evidently their "fight theme" was "*Hook'em Cow.*"
17. Birds: all lithographers and artists back to Louis Prang, have enjoyed drawing birds, but the cigar makers many times tried to incorporate a tie-in to the product or maker. American Litho created a blue jay eating a bee for the J. B. Foster Company's *Jay-Bees* brand and even went one step further with a sign in the background that said: "Foster the habit of buying at Fosters."

The D.A. Schafer Company of Findley, Ohio showed a hummingbird *(Hummer)* feeding on tobacco flowers, and the Grommes and Ullrich Company of Chicago put their *Raven* on top of the book written by Edgar Allen Poe.

The Van Dam Cigar Co. in Grand Rapids, Michigan used a popular cardinal which is the state bird of Illinois, Indiana, Kentucky, North Carolina, Ohio, Virginia and West Virginia. But they opted to call it *Red Bird* as it was more popularly known by the uneducated. Van Dam did squeeze in the reminder that they had been in business since 1893!

The Swann Company of Tampa, Florida merely chose a typical setting for a swan with no gimmicks, but the *Blue Bird* cigar makers felt they needed more so they loaded up the picture with a gold-embossed coat of arms and a few gold metals.

18. The Maryland Litho Co. in Baltimore tried a billy goat titled *Bumper*. Since many people did own goats in those days and probably identified with the appropriate title of *Bumper*.
19. Because of their strength and regal appearances, lions and tigers appeared on a number of products at the turn of the century. *Leo Grande* is a very early non-embossed example, but *Scarlet Crown* created by Schmidt Litho of New York in 1899 pulled out all the stops with heavy gold embossing and a regal crown. *Royal Tigerettes* is a typical example of the high quality of artwork produced by Calvert Litho of Detroit.
20. *The Black Bat* created by Calvert for the Kuhles and Stock Company in St. Paul, Minn. is great art, but I can't imagine it promoting sales!

1. *Alcazar* **
Peter Manning **
Red Tips **
2. *Airedale* **

1.

1.

1.

2.

Montana Sport (English Springer Spaniel) **
Pug ***
El Gaurdo (English Bulldog) **
3. Two Friends ***

3.

2.

2.

3.

TWO FRIEND

2.

*4. Frazzle ****
*5. Elkmont ***
*Double Elk ***

WO FRIENDS

4.

5.

5.

THE SWISHER-ORRISON CO., MAKERS, BETHESDA, OHIO
DOUBLE ELK

6. *Crane's Imported* *
7. *Lone Wolf* **
Big Wolf **
8. *Pig Tail* **
9. *Two Homers* *

6.

8.

7.

9.

TWO HOM
THEY ALWAYS COME
TITLE AND DESIGN REG. IN U.S. PAT. OFF.
2 FOR 5 TWO HOM

7.

10. Our Kitties **
White Cat (reclining) **
White Cat (Puss-In-Boots style) **

10.

10.

Smoke White Cat Cigar.

10.

White-Cat

11. Camel **
12. Two Wheelers ***
13. The Eagle ***
Rex Aguilla ***
14. Henrietta **

11.

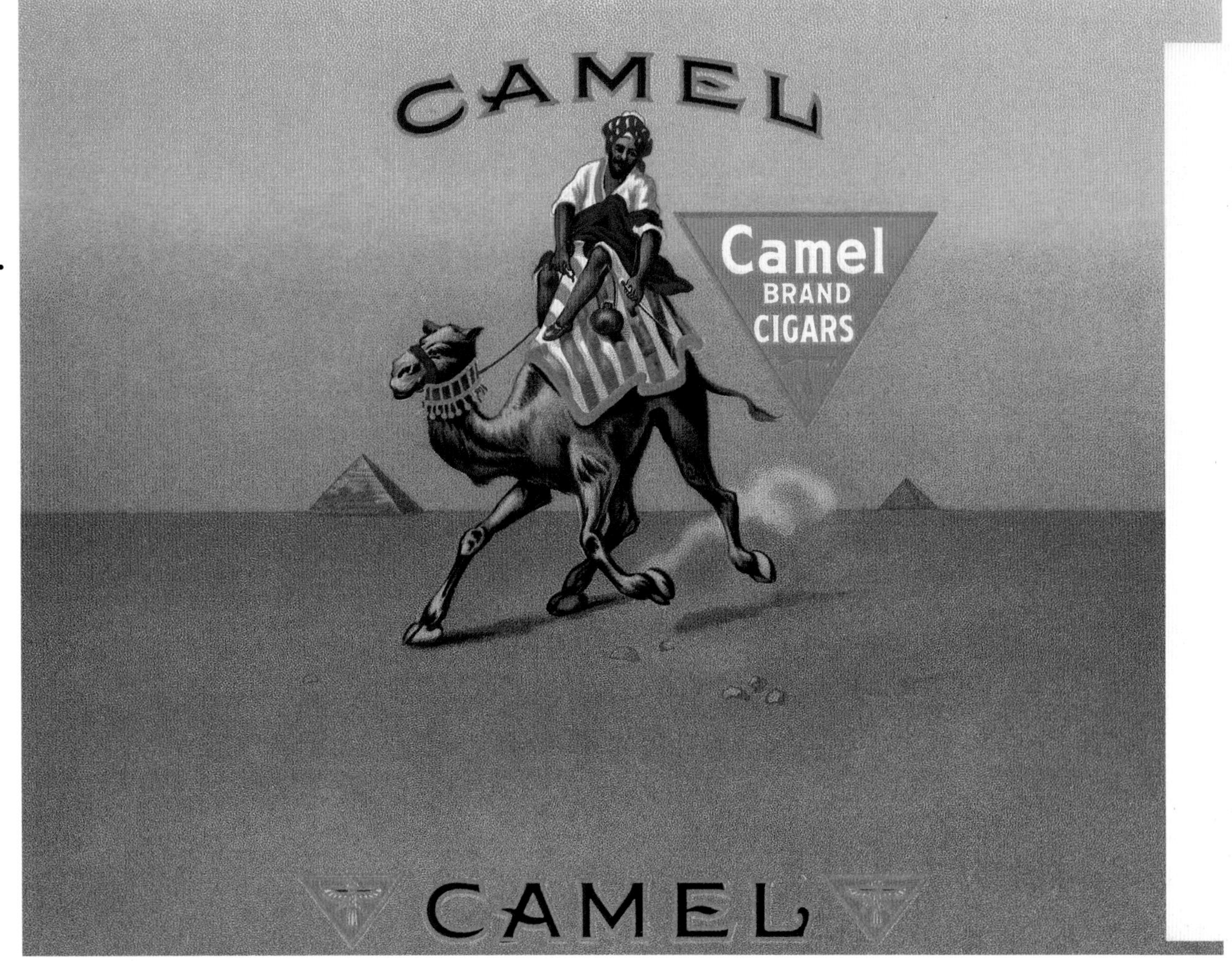

12.

13.

REX AGUILLA

REX AGUILLA

14.

EAGLE

Henrietta
REGISTERED U.S. PAT. OFF.

GLE

13.

15. *Yellow Hornet* **
Buzzer **
16. *Jersey* **
Hook'em Cow **
17. *Jay-Bees* ***
Hummer ***

15.

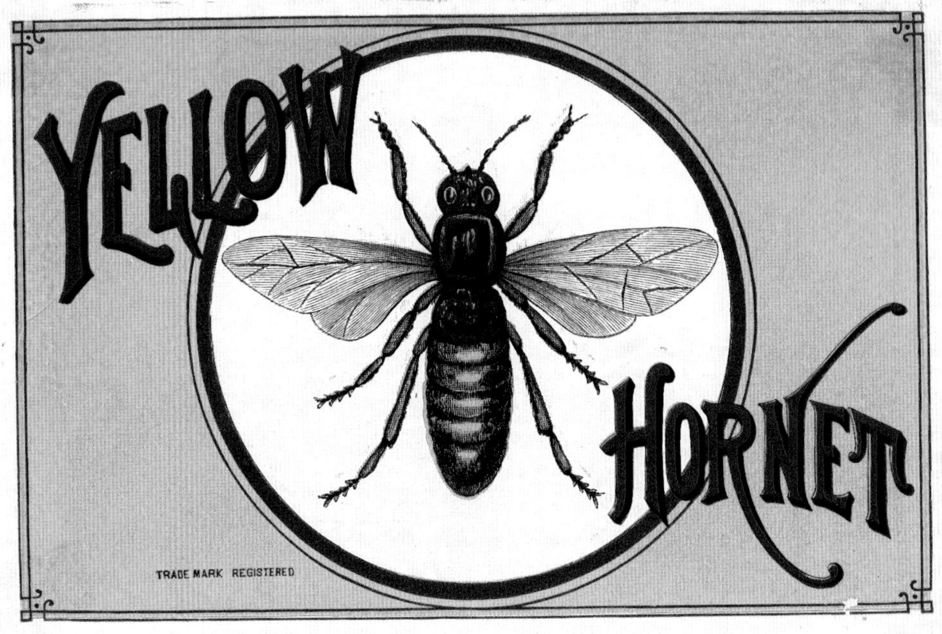

16.

15.

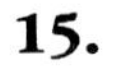

16.

HOOK'EM COW
LET'S GO, LET'S GO, LET'S GO NOW
SO. ST. PAUL CLUB HOOK'EM COW
1916
CIGAR
Copyright by J. C. Verhaag 1921

BAHNEMAN & LIST MAKERS
HOOK'EM COW
ST. PAUL MINN.

17.

SCHAFER'S
HUMMER
MANUFACTURED OF FINEST SELECTIONS
HAVANA AND DOMESTIC TOBACCO

D. A. SCHAFER FINDLAY, O.
HUMMER
HIGH GRADE CIGARS

JAY-BEE'S
FOSTER THE HABIT OF BUYING AT FOSTER'S
JOHN B. FOSTER
JAY-BEE'S
NEWARK, N.J.

17.

Raven **
Red Bird **
Blue Bird **

17.

17.

17.

Swan
*18. Bumper ***
*19. Leo Grande ***

17.

18.

Smoke LEO GRANDE Cigars.

19.

Scarlet Crown **
Royal Tigerettes ***
20. *The Black Bat* ****

19.

20.

19.

SPANISH THEMES

he Spanish West Indies, the birthplace of the hand-rolled cigar, with all its tropical charms and Spanish flavor was an obvious natural for cigar makers to use as a theme for their brands of cigars. As with many of today's products, advertisers liked to tantalize the appetites of the public with the thought that they were purchasing a rare and exotic product from a faraway land. It was an accepted fact that the finest tobaccos have always comc from Cuba and the Spanish West Indies and the use of a Spanish sounding title implied to the purchaser that he was undoubtedly buying the best.

Even when the title was not a Spanish theme, the manufacturer would use such terms as *Fabrica de Tobaccos de la Vuelta Abajo* which meant that the tobacco supposedly was from the Vuelta Abajo province which produced the finest leaves, or simply, *Flor Fina* which was Spanish for "Finest Flower" or "Finest Leaves." Other terms like "Clear Havana" or "100% Pure Havana" somewhere on the main label on top sheet reminded the consumer that they were getting the finest of imported tobacco.

As the domestically grown tobacco industry grew, cost conscious cigar makers started cutting corners by using domestic fillers combined with a clear havana outer leaf wrapper, and a variety of other combinations, and to this day, with over 100,000 cigar makers operating in this country at one time, we will probably never know how many people bought cigars thinking they were imported, but probaly grown in Kentucky or Connecticut.

A prime example of an American Made cigar with a totally Spanish theme is the beautiful, and very popular in its time, is the *La Boda* label which means "The Wedding." It was manufactured in Brazil, Indiana!

1. *Calvano* ••
2. *Captain Alvarez* ••
3. *Corona de Rosas* ••

1.

CALVANO

2.

3.

G.W. CHASE & SON
MERCANTILE CO.

TAMPA
FLORIDA

4. Cuban ••
5. GonzalezSanchez •

4.

5.

6. Havana Favorite •
7. La Balca ••
8. La Boda ••

6.

7.

*9. La Camporita**
*10. La Confesion**

9.

10.

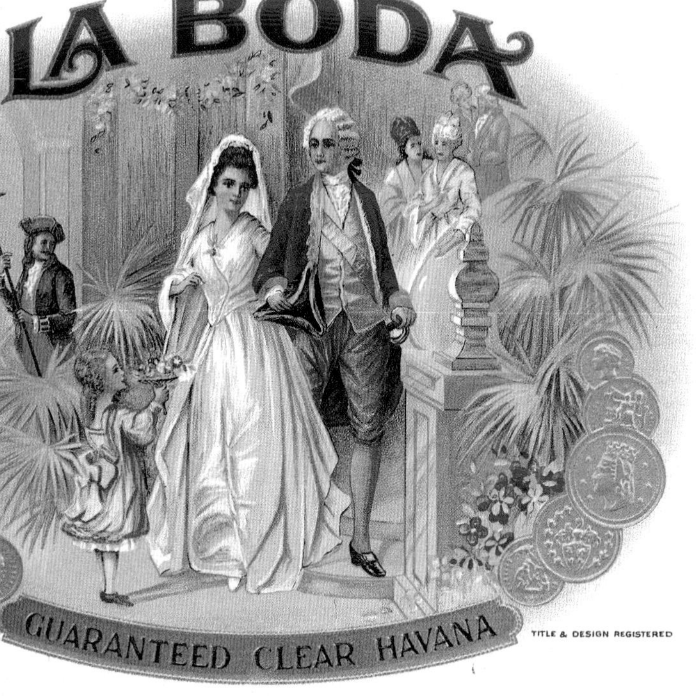

8.

11. La Crownella •
12. La Mia •••
13. La Miretta •

11.

13.

12.

14.

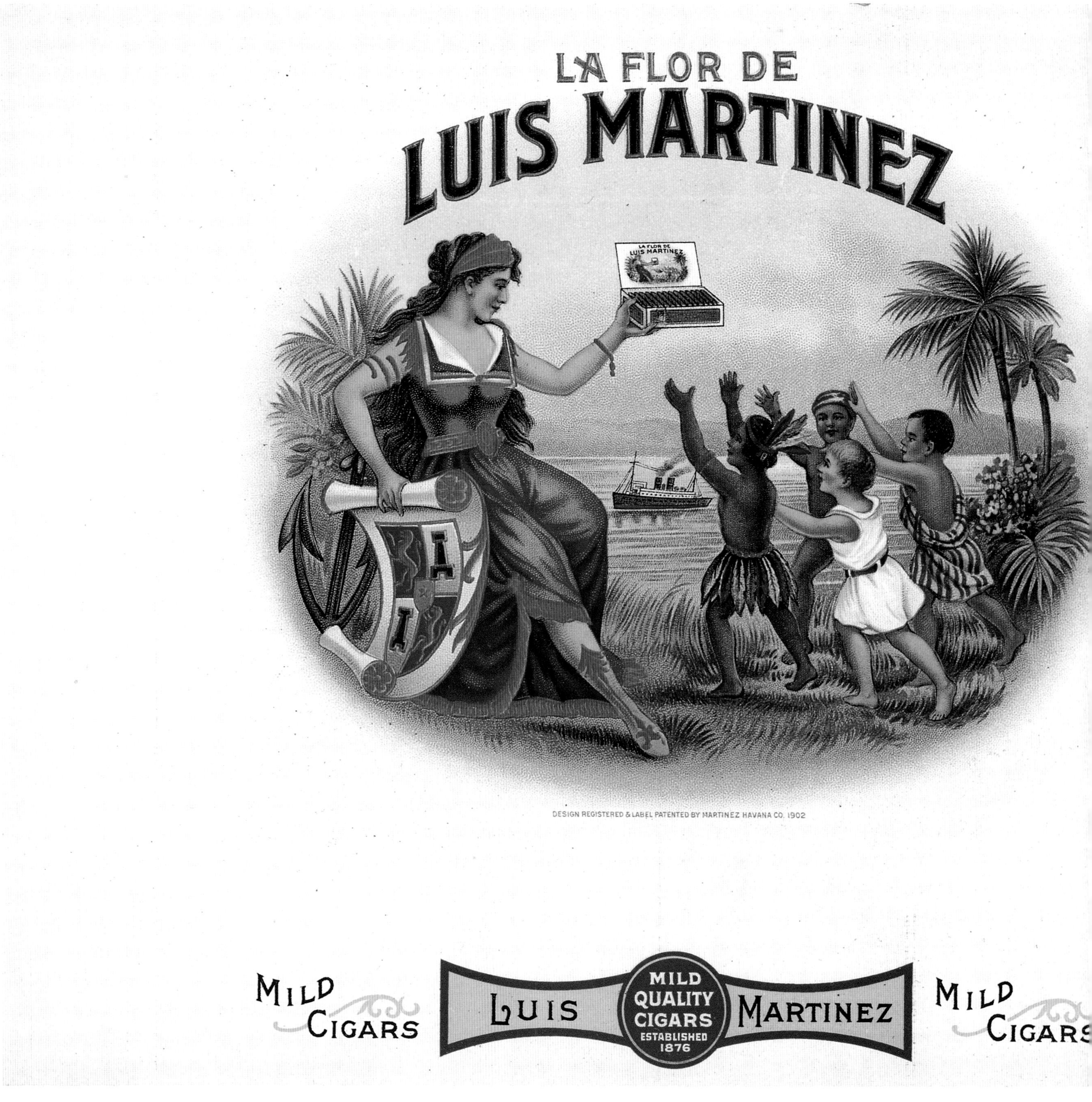
LA FLOR DE
LUIS MARTINEZ
LA FLOR DE LUIS MARTINEZ
DESIGN REGISTERED & LABEL PATENTED BY MARTINEZ HAVANA CO. 1902
MILD CIGARS
LUIS
MILD QUALITY CIGARS ESTABLISHED 1876
MARTINEZ
MILD CIGARS

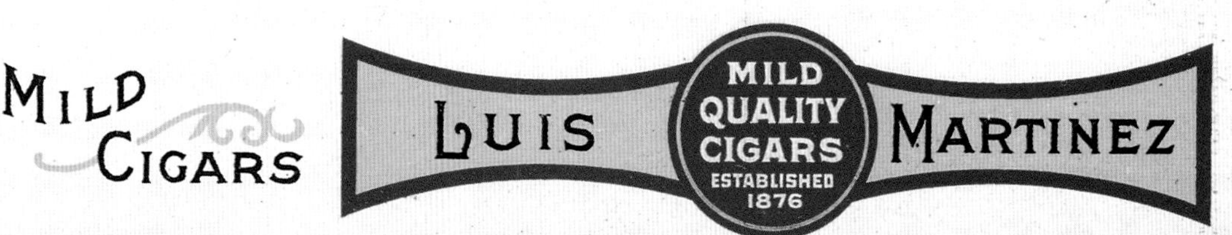

14. Luis Martinez *
15. Merchants Queen **
16. San Julia **

15.

16.

17. Senora Cubana *
18. Spanish Knight **

17.

18.

Foreign labels

My first exposure to what I considered "Foreign" labels was when Joseph Hruby, the band collector sent me a few he had received in his dealings with European band collectors. I was struck by the liberal use of gold leafing on the labels, but could not identify easily with any of the individuals or scenes on these labels since they were mostly Dutch, Belgian, French or Spanish patriots, scenes or buildings. I was obviously pleased to have any new additions to my collection, and relegated them to an album marked "Foreign Labels."

In talking to collectors across the country, over 80% told me that they had little or no interest in "Foreign Labels" in spite of their obvious high quality art and liberal use of gold leaf in many cases. I could never pin them down as to any one specific reason for their rejection, but it could have been a combination of a desire to own labels that only had familiar people or scenes, or that they considered cigar labels as purely Americana, and these just didn't fit in.

What I discovered in my travels and research is that there are "Foreign Labels" and there are "Foreign Labels." Many of the labels you may peruse with European themes, titles or individuals that have found their way to this country were created for the European market and the brands that they promoted were never meant to attract the American cigar smoker. When given a choice between one of these and a label featuring American genre, I obviously would choose the American theme. What I and many other collectors did not know is that foreign lithographers before the World War I blockage contributed a very substantial portion of the cigar labels used in this country with very "American" themes.

German lithographers Moeller-Kokeritz and Klingenberg Litho maintained offices in New York City, Louis Wagner's labels were also created in Germany, and as I mentioned in the chapter on lithographers, both A. B. Henschel and C. B. Henschel of Chicago and Milwaukee were supplied by Klingenberg and others in Germany. Although a major portion of the early American lithographers and artists were German immigrants, the established firms in Germany had an early edge because of their worldwide reputation for quality and the latest technology. I was shocked when I perused the archives of sample labels at Klingenberg Litho in Detmold, Germany and saw many labels I thought were "American." As early as 1880 Klingenberg produced labels featuring Uncle Sam in two versions, titled either *Uncle Sam* or *Yankee*.

One clue that might help you identify European labels is the small notation "Dep. no." below the image. Bernhard von Schubert of Klingenberg Litho told me that this was short for "depose" number which was their method of cataloging the labels by number. Although the designation did not appear on all foreign labels, it certainly helps to identify those that are. There is no doubt that some of the more recent Foreign Labels that have entered this country are certainly easy to spot, but for those of you that are purists and only want American labels in your collection, I'm afraid that you probably already have a number of "Foreign" labels in your collection without even knowing it!

Here are a few examples of labels produced in Germany and Cuba.

1. *Annola:* typical Spanish beauty, but designated for the Klingenberg offices in New York.
2. *Boma:* probably an important black patriot or leader that Europeans knew.
3. *Bouddha:* image of prophet with vignettes of Chinese smoking and playing games. I wonder what they're smoking in those long pipes!
4. *Burgfever:* great artwork with castle burning in background.
5. *Carus-Olympia:* early Olympic hero and chariot races.
6. *Dick-Cop:* I have no idea what message they are trying to convey, but it's different!
7. *Grand Bruxelles:* excellent artwork of major edifices in Brussels, Belgium.
8. *Ivanhoe:* a very popular brand in the U.S., but if you examine it closely, it will show it was printed in Cuba.
9. *Les Deux Soeurs:* two sisters, a theme later copied in the U.S.
10. *Nos Braves:* World War I military scenes.
11. *Rosa Y Yo:* this popular American Brand was one of the very first labels I spotted in the Klingenberg archives.
12. *Sportwereld:* Olympic bust with vignettes of soccer players and bicyclists.
13. *Tom Mix:* although he was world-reknowned, this was produced for American consumption.
14. *Van Dyck:* popular American brand produced by Klingenberg Litho.
15. *Honor et Patria:* spectacular artwork of the monument to Victor Emmanuel in Rome. This is one of the largest labels ever discovered, probably for a box of 250 cigars.
16. *La Confederacion Suiza:* very liberal gold leafing and detail produced in Cuba.
17. *Hertog van Brabant:* knight in armor.
18. *Djibouti:* West Indies street scene
19. *Neumexico:* Mexican label produced in Germany.
20. *Biscops:* goat surrounded by European flags. Not a real motivator in this country!
21. *Verdier*: heavy gold leafed label, produced by Havana Litho in Cuba.
22. *Corvinae*: semi-humorous label, the crows probably depicting the natural wrapper color.
23. *Bleriot*: the French aviator was the first man to fly across the English Channel.

NON-TITLED IMAGES

1. Pope: even popes were featured on labels in Europe. This is Pius the IX.
2. Mexican Cowboy or Bandit: maybe Pancho Villa had a vanity label!
3. Gypsy with Tambourine: gypsies had a certain mystique in Europe.
4. Prince Wilhelm of Germany: spectacular artwork equal to any oil painting.
5. Hunter returning on horseback: hunting of all types was a popular theme on European labels.

UNIQUE 4 X 5 OUTSIDE LABELS

1. *Aeroplane:* a flying cigar, something you would expect from an American artist.
2. *Allright:* bicycle athlete in sepia tone.
3. *Charlemagne:* European conqueror, probably copied from a museum portrait.
4. *Coquette:* Victorian dancing girl.
5. *Reform:* early women's libbers blowing smoke rings.
6. *Radius:* a volcano blowing its top.

*1. Annola ***
*2. Boma ***

1.

2.

*3. Bouddha ****
*4. Burgfever ***
*5. Carus-Olympia ***
*6. Dick-Cop **
*7. Grand Bruxelles ***

3.

4.

5.

6.

8.

*8. Ivanhoe **
*9. Les Deux Soeurs ***
*10. Nos Braves ****

9.

7.

10.

*11. Rosa Y Yo **
*12. Sportwereld ***
*13. Tom Mix ***
*14. Van Dyck ***
*15. Honor et Patria *****
*16. La Confederacion Suiza ***
*17. Hertog van Brabant **

11.

HAVANA ROSA Y YO CIGARS

12.

14.

13.

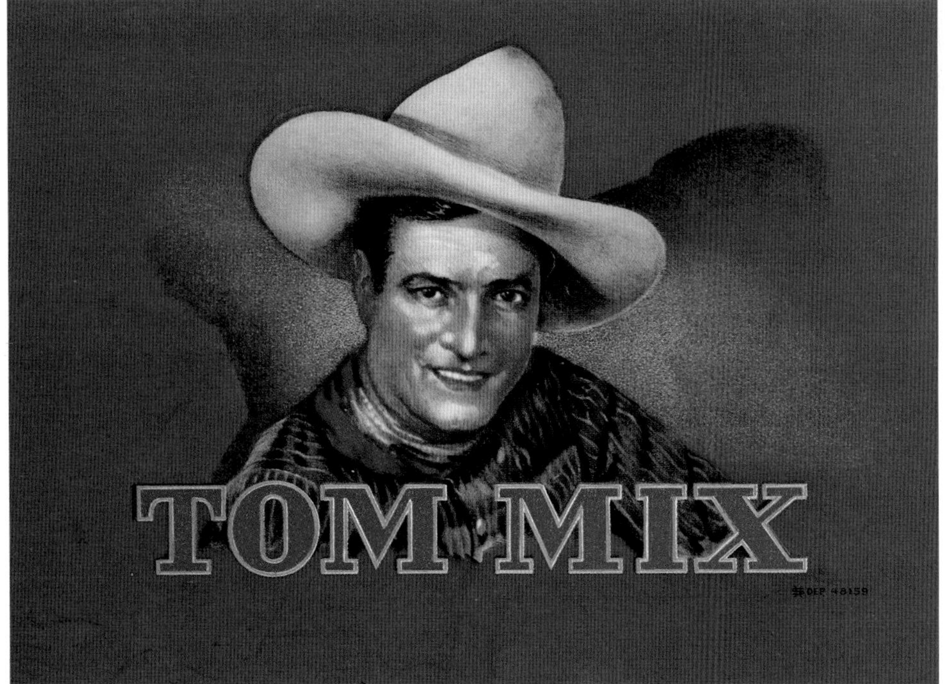

15.

HONORE PATRIA

DYCK
Cigar Co. INC.

16.

17.

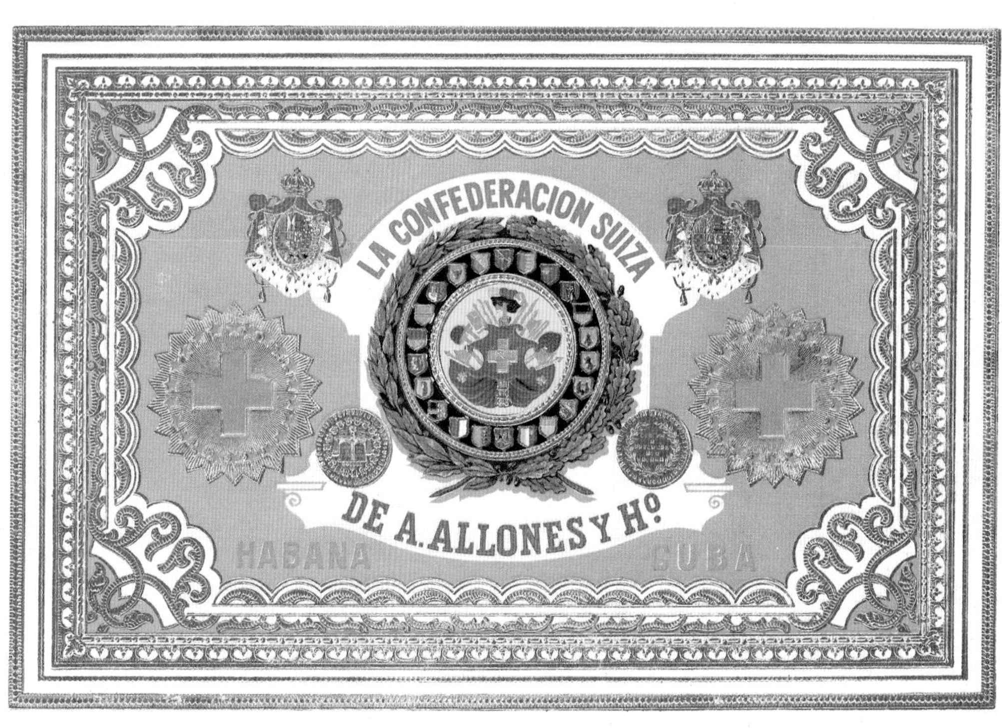
LA CONFEDERACION SUIZA
DE A. ALLONES Y Hº
HABANA
CUBA

*18. Djibouti **
*19. Neumexico **
*20. Biscops **
*21. Verdier ***

18.

19.

20.

BISCOPS

VERDIER
BONDED
CLEAR
HAVANA
CIGARS
COMPAÑIA LITOGRAFICA DE LA HABANA
PRINTED IN CUBA

21.

22. Corvinae **
23. Bleriot ***

NON-TITLED IMAGES
1. Pope **

22.

1.

23.

*2. Mexican Cowboy or Bandit ***
*3. Gypsy with Tambourine **
*4. Prince Wilhelm of Germany ****

2.

3.

4.

*5. Hunter returning on horseback ****

5.

1.

UNIQUE 4 X 5 OUTSIDE LABELS
1. Aeroplane **
2. Allright **
3. Charlemagne **
4. Coquette **

2.

4.

5. Reform **
6. Radius **

5.

6.

VANITY LABELS

anity Labels, a term coined by the printers and boxmakers to describe a label bearing the likeness of the owner, his wife, children or even their pets is physical proof that people don't change very much even after a century of time. Just as you will see today, some poor soul will be making a fool of himself on television trying to promote his used car lot, furniture store or other retail venture. The cigar makers' egos needed the same kind of bolstering, and when they could finally afford it (a custom label start-up could cost $6,000 in 1890) many of them contracted to have their own, or a member of their family's portrait incorporated into the new label design.

One of the most obvious examples that vanity was a factor in the creation of these custom labels was my discovery of some cursive notes appearing on the progressive book for the 1861-Weideman Co. Cigar Label. The label, as you can see from the photograph shows Mr. Weideman, along with the artwork of his old building, his new headquarters, the Oliver Hazard Perry Monument (no explanation for this) and the large 1861, when he started his company. This brand could also be categorized as a "house brand" since the Weideman Company became a large grocery and liquor wholesaler, but because his image also appeared, I have classified it as a vanity label.

When I looked at the final image in the progressive, I felt that it appeared a bit different from the label in my collection, but I couldn't immediately pinpoint the difference. As I thumbed through the pages, I found on one progression, the bold note saying: "Take out the shadows beneath the eyes." with circles in pencil around the bags the artist had reproduced so accurately from Mr. Weideman's picture. A few progressions later, there is a note saying: "Correction has been made." So, the 1861 Weideman label in your collection will show a smooth faced, rosey-cheeked Mr. Weideman, but the original proof showed him with heavy bags under his eyes which Mr. Weideman obviously objected to, and was not going to pay $6,000 to have himself portrayed as such.

Another prominent vanity label, which was produced by Samuel Paley, father of William S. Paley, former president of CBS featured Sam Paley's wife dressed up in a Spanish costume. In an attempt to incorporate the family name into a spanish theme, he gave it the title *La Palina*, a brand which lasted for over 60 years.

Once the photomechanical process came on the scene, costs of vanity labels were reduced dramatically. The lithographers produced labels with blank ovals or squares in the center so the cigar maker's picture could be "dropped" right in, and, although many of the children were quite cute, some of the cigar makers probably harmed their sales by using their own pictures.

1. 1861 Weideman Co. **

1.

2.

2. C.B. Christman Bros. •
3. Champion Antonio •••

3.

4. Girl and boy, green with gold coins **
5. Juliet Perez **
6. Klepfer **
7. La Flor de R. Azogue **

4.

5.

6.

FER
5¢
STRAIGHT
STRAIGHT

7.

LA FLOR DE R. AZOGUE

ET PEREZ
GARANTIZADO
DEL MEJOR TABACO
DE VUELTA ABAJO
ABANA
TRADE MARK REGISTERED

8. Little Joys ••

8.

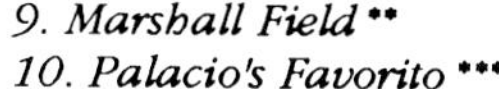

9. Marshall Field **
10. Palacio's Favorito ***

9.

10.

11. Partner **
12. Weingarden's **

11.

12.

NON-PICTORIAL LABELS

bviously, not all cigar labels were pictorial. A large number of dealers chose textual labels, ones depending more on words than pictures to identify their cigars. There were a number of reasons for textual labels. First and foremost, a number of small dealers had a regular and loyal clientele, so there was really no need to purchase the more expensive pictorial labels. "Keep it simple" was also important to some dealers using single letters from "A" to "Z," their own initials like "J.A.C.", or in many cases, the factory number that was assigned to them.

Unfortunately, in my early days of collecting I passed up a number of unique textual labels that I wish I now had. After acquiring a number of different styles in various sample books and small collections, I started to appreciate some of the unique and innovative approaches the artists used to make an attractive textual label.

Labels like *Bank Note* and *Compliments of the Season* are now becoming quite coveted, and since many dealers do not totally appreciate the historical importance of most of these labels compared to their pictorial inventory, there are some great bargains available out there. In most cases, I can grasp the message that the dealer is trying to get across in many of the textual labels, but I really have a problem understanding how a dealer can sell a cigar called *The Pit*.

1. Anthony's Panetela •
2. Aromella •

1.

2.

3. Bank Note ••
4. Bankable •

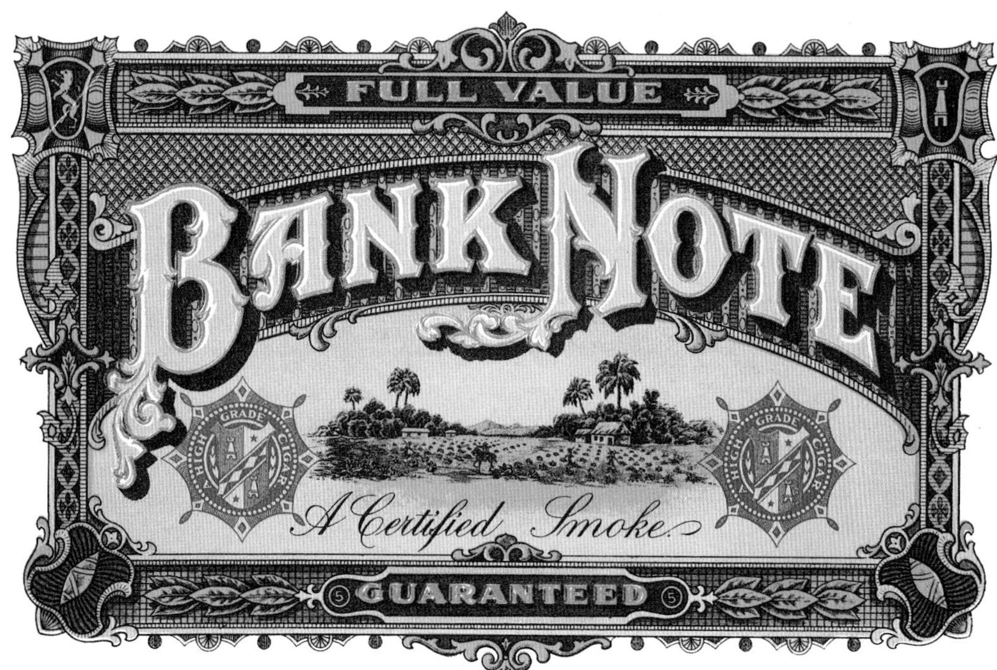

3.

4.

NATIONAL CIGAR CO. BANKABLE

*5. Banker's Bouquet**
*6. Big B Brand**

6.

5.

7. *Big Five**
8. *Bingo**

8.

7.

9. Blue Ribbon •
10. Cambridge ••

9.

10.

11. *Canadian Club**
12. *Choice Made**

11.

12.

13. Club House *
14. Compliments of the Season **

14.

Compliments of the Season

13.

CLUB HOUSE

MILD & SWEET

CLUB HOUSE

15. Conrad's Gold Dollar **
16. Cornwall Arms *

16.

15.

*17. Crown Oak**
*18. Cuban-Americans ***

18.

17.

19. *Echo* •
20. *El Mezzo* •

19.

20.

*21. Eureka**
*22. EV**
*23. Eventual**
*24. F & D**
*25. Five Grand**

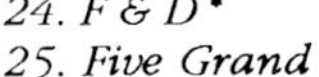

21.

22.

23.

24.

25.

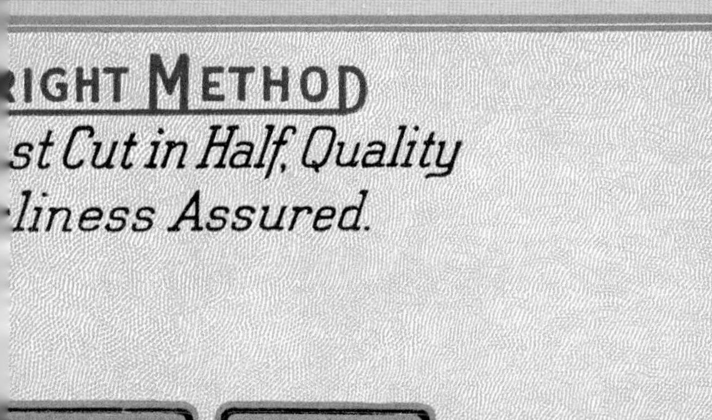

FIVE GRAND

GOOD AS GOLD

TRADE MARK REGISTERED

A LONG BLENDED IMPORTED FILLER

E. B. STRICKLER FIVE GRAND YORK, PA.

*26. Golden Dawn**
*27. Grade "A"**
*28. Harmony**
*29. Inspiration**
*30. J.A.C.**

LONG FILLER **GOLDEN DAWN** HAND MADE

26.

27.

30.

28.

29.

Inspiration

31. *Kennedy's Eureka* •
32. *Kohler's Hand Made* •

31.

32.

33. La Reala Habana **
34. Lydia *

33.

34.

35. New Rose ••
36. Nicki •

36.

35.

39.

GERMANY

*37. Nuggets**
*38. Oxford***
*39. Perfecto Garcia***

37.

38.

40. Porto Habana •
41. Prudential •

40.

41.

42. Queen Seal•
43. Saeger's Monogram•
44. Saeger's Single Binder•

43.

44.

42.

45. Sinceridad •
46. Standard Quality-High Grade •
47. The Pit ••
48. Vale •
49. Veto •
50. Vico •

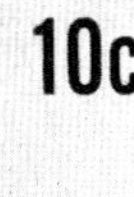

45.

46.

48.

VALE
TRADE MARK REGISTERED

VALE
CIGAR

49.

VETO
THIS 5¢ CIGAR VETOES
THE NECESSITY OF PAYING
10¢ FOR A GOOD SMOKE.

47.

50.

FABRICA DE TABACOS
HABANA VICO CIGARS

*51. Victory***
*52. Welwel**

51.

52.

STOCK LABELS

tock Labels, specifically labels already printed with only the title missing (which could be easily added by hand letterpress) were a bonus for the small cigar makers who could never afford the more expensive specially ordered labels. By merely choosing a pre-printed label from the salesman's sample book which the cigar maker felt would enhance his image or fit into his market place, he could order as few as 100 labels at a time without any up front expenses, or having to commit to minimum orders in excess of 10,000 labels.

As you can see from the examples, the Milaca Cigar Company of St. Paul, Minnesota called this attractive young lady *Lady Huntley*. While down in Florida, her image was used by the Miami Club. Frank Hazinski, of South Bend, Indiana, chose this exotic looking lady pictured with a Middle East skyline in the background and named her *Alcinta* while another manufacturer gave it the rather inappropriate title of *Chapman House*.

By looking at the various untitled stock labels in this section, I'm sure that you can choose some quite appropriate titles for most of them, but I'm sure that the stock label created by the imaginative American Litho artists showing a girl perched on the point of a steeple might need a bit more imagination!

1. Alcinta •
2. Boy smoking with puppies looking over fence •••
3. Chapman House •
4. Girl perched on steeple •••

1.

FRANK HAZINSKI SOUTH BEND, IND.

3.

2.

4.

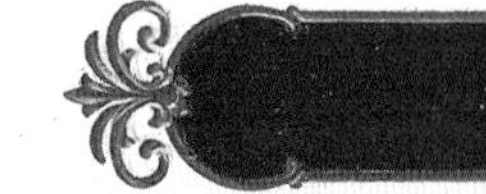

5. *Girl with wings & children & topless dancer***
6. *Lady Huntley**

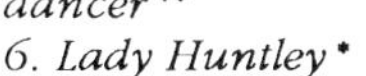

5.

6.

*7. Man peeking around corner at girl***
*8. Miami Club**
*9. Open panel with cherubs**

7.

8.

9.

11.

10. Red lion & workers in field *
11. Smoke the Celebrated ___ Cigars **
12. Three men drinking & toasting **

172

10.

12.

13. Woman & fan **
14. Woman on sofa putting on garter **
15. Nobleman surrounded by cigar boxes *
16. Kittens on red stockinged leg ***

13.

14.

15.

16.

SAMPLE LABELS

Spurred by the dramatic growth of the cigar industry in the 1890's, lithographers and label brokers encouraged their creative staffs to generate more and more new images and themes. Many of the new cigar makers might be set up in a basement of their home, or in a cottage in the rear, but to compete with the larger factories, they needed to project a certain "look" or identify with an important person, place or favorite pastime. Just like our ad agencies today, the lithographers and label brokers needed samples of their work for the use of their salesmen in the field, for their showrooms, and in direct mail campaigns in which they sent small sample books to cigar makers who had recently been assigned a tax number with the federal government. The directories and new listings provided an inexpensive mail order list!

Sample labels that you will run across in your travels were displayed in about six different formats, and if you own a single sample label, it probably came from one of these. The largest assemblage of samples usually came in a boxmaker's sample book, which weighed over 30 pounds. This type of book contained hundreds of images that had already been chosen by a dealer to place on his clients' boxes. The images were made by various lithographers and had the cigar maker's name and the date written in longhand at the bottom. Since the labels in the boxmaker's sample book had actually been chosen, registered and put into production, you can be assured that a quantity of them existed.

Two other types of "heavyweight" sample books were kept in the possession of the lithographer. One, used by the printing foreman, was kept in the back of the shop, and was used in a way similar to the boxmaker's book. It was a visual record of the client's images, with the name, the date the label was initiated, and a date when the image was removed from the stone. In some cases, devastating to the label collector, the foreman crayoned a large black "X" through the image when it was no longer used.

The other type of these books was typically more elaborate, with hand-tooled covers and gold embossing, and was kept in the showroom to display to prospective clients. It contained a variety of "stock" images, some with only the image and no title, as well as a large variety of newer images and those not yet chosen by clients. All of the three above "heavyweights" ordinarily contained from 500 to 800 images.

Again, an important point to remember is that boxmaker's *and* foreman's books with handwritten notations were actually put into production. Although you and I may never see another label like those pictured, the fact remains that a quantity was produced, probably being put on the boxes, or being destroyed when the cigar maker went out of business.

A smaller sample book *(O.L. Schwencke Book* pictured*)* was given to the company salesmen and label brokers. Usually leather-bound and embossed with gold, containing from 80 to 100 images, these books in their original state are highly coveted by collectors, because many of today's dealers have broken them apart to sell the labels individually. An appropriate analogy for all of you art lovers: finding one of these books intact would be like finding a bound volume of original Audubons!

Still another format for distributing samples was the "mini-book" *(*pictured*)* used by lithographers in their direct mail campaigns. Usually containing from six to twelve images, tens of thousands of them were mailed to old and new customers alike. More of these books have survived, but they are rapidly being broken up by dealers to sell single labels.

Individual sample sets (pictured) with the inner and outer labels and the trim stapled together were turned out in large quantities, primarily by German lithographers. While some American firms used them, American lithographers in general felt that the sample books gave a far more professional presentation.

As you can see from some of the samples pictured, the lithographers printed their names and addresses directly on the samples they sent out. Until competition became more aggressive, they even printed prices for quantities of 100, 1,000 or more right on the labels.

Because of confidence in their creative abilities and pride in workmanship, and with such innovations as embossing, gold leafing, and bronzing to make their labels more attractive, price was not a major concern at first, and there were no "discounters" around as there are today. But as more and more lithographers jumped on the lucrative cigar label bandwagon, and the high turnover rate among the "Mom and Pop" cigar makers, some lithographers finally succumbed to discounting as a matter of survival.

I believe every collector should have at least a few examples of cigar label samples to round out their collection, because this is an example of one step in the total process.

There are a number of factors to take into consideration when you are purchasing or collecting samples. Looking at them from the standpoint of rarity and investment, obviously the samples of images that were never chosen by a cigar maker are rarer than those that went into production. But, keep in mind, that the lithographers cranked out many thousands of samples during their mail order campaigns. So, considering the survival rate, there may be many more rare individual labels than samples in existence. Recent auction records show that single labels such as *Fellow Citizens, Lime Kiln Club, Captain January* and *Frontier* have brought prices from $125 to $400 while some sample labels in the same auction have gone as little as $20.

1.

*1. Bible Class, F. Heppenheimer & Sons *****
*2. Curly Locks, Louis C. Wagner Co. ****

2.

3. Good Prospects, Schumacher & Ettinger **
4. La Reina de Las Vegas, Louis E. Neuman & Co. **
5. La Salle, A.C. Henschel Co. **

3.

4.

5.

6. *Liberty Light, F. Heppenheimer's Sons* ***
7. *Little Pet, Schmidt & Co.* ***
8. *Merry Christmas-Happy New Year, Schmidt & Co.* ****

6.

7.

8.

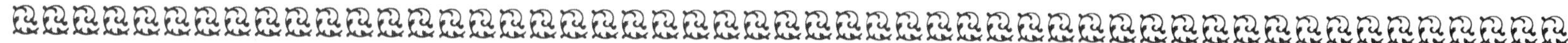

9. Mrs. Jack Frost, Schmidt & Co. ****
10. Ocean Belle, Johns & Co. ***
11. Queen Dolly, Heywood, Strasser, Voigt Litho Co. ***

9.

11.

No. 520 — Inside .... $ 3.20 per 100 } also
No. 521 — Outside .... „ 1.50 „ 100 } blank.
Heywood, Strasser & Voigt Litho C
155–161 Leonard St., New-York. 160 Washington St., Chicago, Il

10.

Ocean Belle

Also Blank.
Ins No. 1612, Outs No. 1613.
$20.00 per 1000. $2.20 per 100. $10.00 per 1000 $1.10 per 100.
Johns & Co.,
21 to 39 Perkins' Power Block, Cleveland O.
215 Bowery, cor. Rivington St. New York City.

*12. Royal Match, Witsch & Schmitt ***
*13. White Crow, C.B. Henschel Co. ****
14. Large Sample Book, Klingenberg Litho

12.

WITSCH & SCHMITT,
94 Bowery, New York.

No. 1106 ins., No. 1107 outs.
ALSO BLANK.

14.

15. Small Sample Books, Moller, Kokeritz, Neuman, Schlegel
16. O.L. Schwenke Sample Book

15.

16.

TRIMMINGS

rimming was a word used by the people in the cigar industry to describe all the standard paper labeling to be glued or attached to a box of cigars. Obviously, the most popular and best known is the approximately 6" x 9" artwork glued to the inner side of the lid. Since it was the largest of the "Trimmings" and usually had the largest image, it was coveted as a frameable artwork, and also fit easily into album pages for collectors. The next most popular trim item is the end label, used on the outside of the box which was usually 4 1/2" x 4 1/2" when all boxes contained 100 cigars, and later was reduced to 2" x 5" for 50 cigar boxes.

Also applied to the outside of the box (usually on the bottom) was the caution notice created by an Act of Congress in 1868 because small cigar stores were caught refilling empty cigar boxes with cigars on which no tax had been paid, and this was a reminder of the penalties for the abuse of the law. These are certainly not as attractive or frameable, but are a plus if you want to have all the trimmings from one brand. Also glued to the outside of the box was the "nail tag," used to cover up the nail that sealed the box. As long as this attractively lithographed seal had not been broken, it was a form of guarantee that the lid had not been opened, and the contents were guaranteed to be of the quality promised by the manufacturer.

They were sometimes called "signature tags" because they often read: "None Genuine without the Signature of ___." Another symbolic gesture by the manufacturer to guarantee the contents were sealed at the factory. Nail tags come in a variety of shapes, from ovals to squares to triangles, are usually quite attractive and frame up well individually or in montages. The edging strips were added decoration to cover up the muslin hinge that attached the lid to the box. The more expensive edging usually carried out the theme of the other trimmings, but there were stock edgings available ranging from plain white to mosaic designs at much lower costs.

Almost all of these outside trimmings became obsolete with the introduction of cardboard boxes and a total paper "box-wrap" which was in one piece and could be applied by machinery. Back inside the box are the "top sheet," 6" x 9" in size and used to lay on top of the cigars. It is the same size as the decorative inner label, but has much less elaborate artwork and it is sometimes mistaken as the lid label. These were almost immediately discarded upon opening the box.

By the turn of the century, the more promotional minded manufacturers who were aware of the collectibility of the bands started making top sheets out of felt with all kinds of images from flags to sports figures. The wives of these cigar smokers started sewing them into quilts and pillowcases, and some of these surface from time to time at antique shows and flea markets. The final "trimming" for the box is the "back tag" which was glued to the back of the box and usually repeated the subject theme but was an extra expense for the cigar maker and many of the smaller dealers omitted them completely.

So here you have all of the basic trimmings as pictured for the *Justin Morrill* set (he was founder of the Republican Party), and you can also see that although it is certainly great to have a complete set, that the 6" x 9" inner label and the 4 1/2" x 4 1/2" outer end label are certainly the most attractive and desirable.

This can also serve as a graphic reminder that when the shady dealers offer "50 labels for $20.00" you could be getting a lot of back flaps, top sheets and caution notices in the load! In an effort to show you some of the diversity of theme and imaginative designs used in the outer labels, here are a few examples.

1. *American Citizen* •
2. *American Protectorate* •
3. *Archimedes* ••

2.

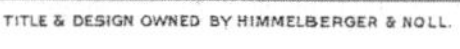

1.

3.

4. Be A Man•
5. Bingo•
6. Castle Hall•
7. Christy Girl••
8. Clipper••
9. Covered Wagon•
10. Cuban•
11. Double Elk•

12. Elkmont *
13. Exposition **
14. Fellow Citizens ***
15. Flor de Scotia **
16. Gov. Chase *
17. Grauley *
18. Grey Horse *
19. Hartmann's Wish *

12.

13.

14.

15.

16.

17.

18.

19.

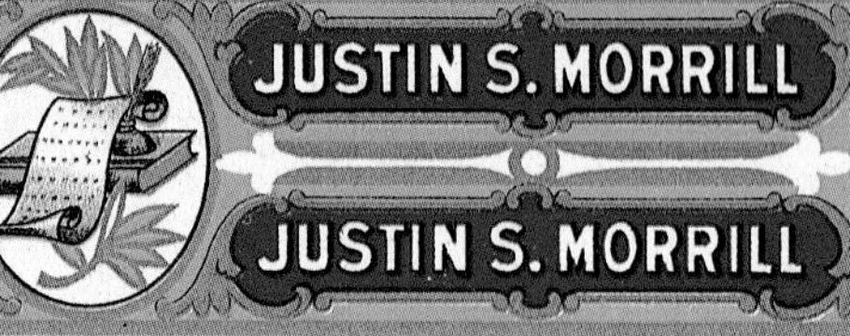

23.

20. Huyler•
21. Illinois Club House•
22. J. Sterling Morton•
23. Justin Morrill Set••••

20.

21.

E.H.HICKS.

22.

J. STERLING MORTON

J. STERLING MORTON

DESIGN COPYRIGHTED 1903 BY SAEGER & SONS, FREMONT NEB. THE MOEHLE LITHO CO. BROOKLYN N.Y.

23.

23.

FACTORY No. 90, 10TH DISTRICT, OHIO.

NOTICE: THE MANUFACTURER OF THE CIGARS HEREIN CONTAINED HAS COMPLIED WITH ALL THE REQUIREMENTS OF LAW. EVERY PERSON IS CAUTIONED NOT TO USE EITHER THIS BOX FOR CIGARS AGAIN, OR THE STAMP THEREON AGAIN, NOR TO REMOVE THE CONTENTS OF THIS BOX WITHOUT DESTROYING SAID STAMP UNDER THE PENALTIES PROVIDED BY LAW IN SUCH CASES.

23.

TITLE & DESIGN REGISTERED BY MAKER.

23.

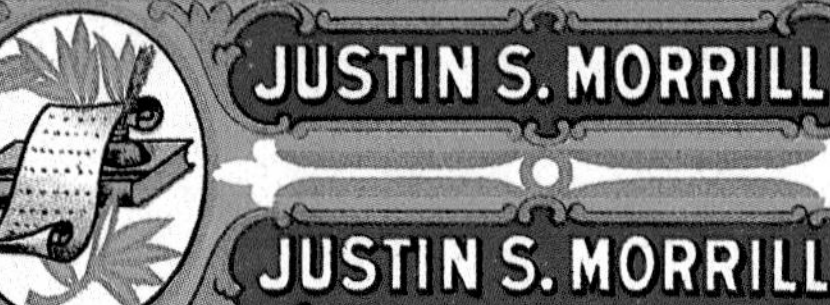

23.

24. *Knickerbocker* •
25. *La Cantarina* ••
26. *La Flor de Lincoln* ••
27. *La Rochelle* •
28. *Lady Mary* •
29. *Little African* ••

30. *Mapacuba* **
31. *Old Abe* *
32. *Paid In Full* **
33. *Paul Dudley* *
34. *Pony Post* **

30.

31.

32.

33.

34.

35. Rex Aquilla •
36. Sallie Slick •
37. Scarlet Crown •
38. Sherlock Holmes •
39. Shrine ••
40. Silver Lace ••
41. Silver Prince •

35. 36. 37. 38. 39. 40. 41.

42. *Sophomore* •
43. *Temple* •
44. *The Raven* •
45 *Tom Hendricks* ••
46. *Twilight Club* •
47. *Vaudeville Sports* ••
48. *Walt Whitman* ••

42.

43.

44.

45.

46.

47.

48.

49. War Chest[**]
50. Wedding Scene[*]
51. White Orchid[*]
52. White Thief[***]
53. You Need the Doctor[**]

CIGAR BANDS

An entire book could be written about collecting cigar bands, a hobby enjoyed by millions at the turn of the century. Band collecting played an important part as the predecessor of cigar label collecting. There are many stories about the origin of cigar bands, but it seems well established that bands originated in Cuba. One story is that cigar makers were obliged to put a paper ring around the cigars in order to protect the fingers of the many ladies who smoked cigars and complained about nicotine stains on their fingers. Another version says that a prominent cigar manufacturer, discovering that some unscrupulous individuals were manufacturing cigars with inferior tobacco under his name, designed a colorful ring identifying each of his cigars in the box; the idea caught on, and other reputable manufacturers began to do the same. Existing bands go back as far as 1870, but it is known from Cuban archives that the first bands were issued in the 1830's.

As we know, most "collectors" start at an early age. The intensity and passion of our young people is evident in today's collectible world by the multi-million dollar industries in baseball cards, comic books and toys. Children at the turn of the century had the deep-rooted desire to collect things but neither the product nor the money was available in those times. So children then had to get very basic and collect what was available as well as attractive to them.

What *was* available in great supply were sidewalks and gutters littered with beautiful multi-colored, gold embossed cigar bands courtesy of the millions of cigar smokers of the era, who usually discarded the band when they unwrapped their cigars outside the store. Since Porches, Yuppie ties and Rolex watches hadn't arrived on the scene as status symbols, smoking a cigar was the "in" thing to give a successful appearance, and with the proliferation of cigars came the ready supply of the attractive, collectible and free cigar bands for the kids.

Fierce competition among the thousands of cigar makers motivated the lithographers to create more and more unique designs and images. This brought into being an open-ended and expanding collectible never before seen in the ephemera field.

Although the lithographers concentrated on the major artwork, which was the inner label that was exposed when the box was opened for display in the cigar case, they usually tried to create a smaller pictorial image of the person, animal, building or other subject on the band. This practice died out after War World I when, as in many industries, price unfortunately won out over quality and workmanship. Lithographers, at the request of cigar makers, began to replace the pictorial images on bands with simply a name, initial or embossed logo.

However, cigar makers and lithographers had gotten the word, early in the century, of the collecting craze among those kids, who were now growing up and becoming cigar smokers. So they started to create "sets" of cigar bands, many of which never appeared on cigars. There were presidential sets, state sets, animal sets, and on and on. Since these sets were sold at retail as collectibles, lithographers once again could give rein to their creativity and artistic abilitities, without being hindered by price conscious small manufacturers. Cigar makers got some mileage out of the used bands by setting up a premium program, in which the smoker would send in his old bands for premium gifts ranging from a three-pack of cigars up to a humidor.

The large inner and outer cigar labels in pristine condition, which we now discover from time to time, never reached the cigar box. They were sent out in sets to creative and industrious young people who were too impatient to scavenge the streets and alleys for bands and who took the initiative to write to cigar makers and lithographers. For some reason the manufacturers were very kind to these young collectors, sending them entire sets, which included not only the bands, but all the inner and outer labels and trim, at no charge. I imagine that they thought of this as a way to get the image of their products into the public eye; little did they know that they were creating a collectible of the future.

I consider myself very fortunate to have interviewed such early collectors as the late Ed Kilcline and a couple of dedicated "kids" who have been collecting for well over a half a century: Joseph J. Hruby of Ohio and Louis Van Duren of Belgium.

Although you will see ads and requests for cigar bands from time to time in the antique and ephemera publications around the country, cigar band collecting was decimated by a number of events, including the demise of many of the older and more advanced collectors, and the greatly decreased number of American cigar manufacturers since 1945.

More dramatic was the campaign by the anti-smoking groups, which brought negative connotations to anything relating to tobacco. Interestingly enough, the rest of the civilized world doesn't seem so be so intent on taking the last few pleasures away from people; smoking and all its paraphernalia are quite well accepted throughout Europe, the Middle East and Asia. A European doctor once mused that it was interesting that Americans were so fearful of "secondary smoke" when they drink water that "has over 100 carcinogens in it, can't go outside on smoggy days and pop millions of tranquilizer pills in an effort to obtain the results probably derived from a good cigar." So, as most of Europe and Asia keep puffing away, cigar band collecting has not dwindled one iota, with the ranks of Spanish, French, Belgian and German collectors growing every year.

ORIGINAL ART

At the peak of the Golden Age of cigar label art, an army of fine and talented artists toiled in dimly lit offices or perhaps seated in large workrooms under a supervisor's stern gaze creating millions of complex, beautiful and inspirational designs in an effort to persuade the millions of cigar smokers to buy a particular brand. Many of these would come to be recognized as masterpieces of the advertising illustrators art. Less than 10% of the artworks submitted ever made it to the stones in the flatbed press, but sometimes the art directors would keep a quantity of artworks in a file for possible future use, and these are probably the only examples that have survived today. Whenever a discovery of original art for cigar labels was found, such as the hoard from Eastern Colortype in the last few years, and the collection donated to the art gallery of Windsor in Canada in 1982, it has usually been in quantities of over 100. In some cases, they were discovered among old files, during major moves or buy-outs and usually thrown away, but thankfully some employees with an eye for good art carted them home to be saved, or sold them to antique dealers at reasonable prices.

What was confusing to the cigar label collectors who ended up with some of them was the fact that they couldn't find the label to match the artwork. Not realizing that most of the original artworks found never reached the lithographing stage, I and many other collectors of cigar art searched relentlessly to find any labels that may match our artworks.

In 1982, I was contacted by the curators of the Art Gallery of Windsor, Canada to come up and view a collection of original art that was donated to them by Mrs. Wallace R. Campbell, widow of the Chairman of Ford Motor Company of Canada. One of their reasons for contacting me was their hope that I might have a label or had seen a label that matched any of their artworks. Upon examining the artworks, I discovered that most of them were registered to the Calvert Litho Company of Detroit with a few from Schlegel Litho, William Steiner, Passbach-Voice and Heywood, Strasser Voigt, all of New York.

It was a great pleasure to view any artifacts from the golden age of cigars and especially thrilling to view artworks created by Calvert Litho, whose history I did not start researching until 1983. Much to my disappointment, I found no duplicate of anything I had ever owned or seen, and I now realize that with most surviving artworks that will generally be the rule. That is not to say that no original art for existing labels does not exist, since I did see examples in the Klingenberg Archives in Germany. But the chances of you or I acquiring such a plum is rather remote.

There are not enough recorded sales to establish a firm benchmark for values of original art, but, as with labels themselves, you can be assured that the subject matter of the art should definitely affect the value. The last piece of original cigar art I witnessed for sale at auction in 1987 went for $150, and was what I would consider "average." Had it been an Indian Chief or baseball player, I'm sure that price would have tripled. The original art pictured here from Calvert Litho is a typical attempt at another Spanish theme with no title assigned and probably never made it as a label.

PROOFS

Whether producing a limited edition artwork or new can label design, the artist or printing production manager always runs a few "proofs" after deciding on a final layout, design or color mix. This allows them to critique the work and to correct any slight imperfections that may not be pleasing to the eye of the potential customer. If you own a cigar label proof, you already know that proofs have registration marks* prominently displayed, and they are never embossed.

The purpose of the registration marks on each proof (marks which also appear on each stone) is to assure that each run, be it the first, second or even twenty-second, aligns perfectly. This keeps the proper mix of shading in the stipple dots and makes sure that the subject doesn't appear to be cross-eyed or blurred.

Proofs are not embossed because that step is not critical to the proofreading which is concerned with color mix and registration. The areas to be embossed are already designated; for example, a flat gold area is shown where coins or medals will be embossed. The proof also usually displayed a series of "color bars" as shown on the examples displayed, which is a simple method of showing exactly how many colors were used.

Any proofs that have survived have come from records and files of those old lithographers who seemingly kept everything forever. Unfortunately, many, many more were destroyed when a particular cigar brand died off. So proofs are obviously very rare. Auction records show price ranges from $35 to $500, with most in the $75 to $125 range. To round out your collection, it would be nice to have at least one proof; even better would be to have a proof of a label that you also own!

1. *Highland Reel* ****
2. *Man Wrestling Lion* ****
3. *Red Glare* ****
4. *Tormenta* ****

PROGRESSIVES

If you ever wanted to add a crown jewel to your collection, you'd have to consider a progressive! Not only is it a one-of-a-kind; it's a complete assemblage of every run of every stone, on its own page, progressing to, and including, the finished product. A very modest quantity of progressives is known to have survived in pristine condition, since most of them endured considerable wear and tear because of the printer's need to refer to them frequently. Also, they were often disassembled by the antique dealers or "diggers" who found them and didn't realize the historical or intrinsic value of the complete arrangement. Tearing out the last two or three progressions, the dealers sold them as labels or proofs for $50 to $75 each, not knowing they would have been worth more than tenfold that amount if the book were intact!

The lion's share of progressives known to survive are now housed in museums and in college library collections. But let me remind you, that many people thought all the cigar labels that could be found had been discovered by 1979, yet there have been four to six major discoveries per year since then, so I am sure more progressives will surface!

I was very fortunate to have acquired a few progressives when I purchased the surviving contents of the Calvert Litho Company of Detroit. Since I paid a lump sum for everything, there was no specific valuation assigned to the progressives in that transaction. However, I did pay $1,000 for the *1861–Weideman* progressive in 1983; primarily because Mr. Weideman started his company in my home town, it was a vanity label, and I have one of the stones, so to me that was a real bargain!

I have seen progressives sell for as little as $250 at a poorly attended auction, but I fear that events like that are few and far between. A more realistic range would be from $500 to $1500 if the subject was sports, animals, cowboys, Indians, Negroes or transportation. In terms of valuation, the subject matter is obviously an important determinant, but the number of progressions and the reputation of the lithographer are also factors.

I still remember the dealer who predicted that no cigar label would be worth more than $7.00, and who, three years later, offered to sell me one for $400. Any effort to convince me that collectibles no longer set new records will fall on deaf ears, ever since the day my son showed me that the Mickey Mantle rookie card I once owned is now worth $5,500!

Paul Mayo progressive from Calvert Litho.

PAUL MAYO
PAUL MAYO
Vuelta Abajo
Habana
Fábrica de Tabacos
de la
MAYO'S PLANTATION.
Habana
PAUL MAYO
PAUL MAYO
Habana

PAUL MAYO
PAUL MAYO
9332
PAUL MAYO
PAUL MAYO
Habana
14697
PAUL MAYO
PAUL MAYO
Habana
14758
PAUL MAYO
PAUL MAYO
Vuelta Abajo
15095
PAUL MAYO
PAUL MAYO
Vuelta Abajo
Habana
PAUL MAYO
PAUL MAYO
Vuelta Abajo
Habana

PAUL MAYO
PAUL MAYO
Fabrica de Tabacos
de la
Vuelta Abajo
MAYO'S PLANTATION.
Habana

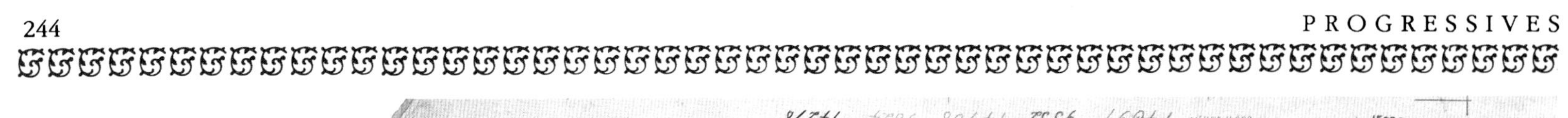

PAUL MAYO

PAUL MAYO

Fabrica de Tabacos

de la

Vuelta Abajo

MAYO'S PLANTATION.

Habana

Fabrica de Tabacos

14776

HISTORICAL ART

In the golden age of cigar label art, literally thousands of subjects were used to attract the eyes and nickels of our forefathers. Since most cigars were smoked by men, it is no surprise that the various themes shown on the labels were what the lithographers thought men liked. Used as a historical record, men liked pretty ladies, patriotism, sports, cowboys and Indians, animals, famous people and various forms of transportation, not necessarily in that order. They also provide us with an insight into the culture of that era, reflecting the values and spirit of the times. They picture a man's world, a Victorian world, with idealized images of reality. You see pictures of a proud and patriotic America, a time when achievements and heroes were admired and celebrated. You also get a glimpse of their humor and their sly double-entendres which still make you laugh today. We can see what the people wore, from hairstyles to shoe styles, their hobbies, and the leisure pastimes they enjoyed.

In depicting minorities, those featuring Negroes were generally humorous and insulting, the Chinese were depicted as something less than human, and the Irish in many cases as drunken bums. The red man, on the other hand was usually shown as a noble warrior, possibly because he no longer remained a threat to us and our politicians had already taken anything of possible value from them.

Using appeal-to-pride psychology, many labels associated cigar smoking with the good times, showing ladies and gentlemen of the upper class known as "swells" or "dandies," attending parties and living the high life in lavish surroundings. After the Depression began, few cigar makers were anxious to picture such lifestyles on the working man's cigars.

Additional themes that were used in quantity:

Patriotism
War
Home Life
Pretty Maidens
Nudes
Children
Chaste Women
Cowboys
Indians
Negroes
Chinese
Spaniards
Plantations
Kings
Generals
Explorers
Heroes
Presidents
Writers
Doctors & Nurses
Actors
Actresses
Poets
Educators
Philosophers
Economists
Gods
Religious Figures
Mythology
Fictional Characters
Cherubs
Comic Strip Characters
Caricatures
Bicycles
Ships

Aviation
Baseball
Football
Soccer
Fishing
Horse Racing
Hunting
Gambling
Uncle Sam
Flags
Birds
Fish
Animals
Reptiles
Maps
Dancers
Buildings & Factories
Christmas
Country Life
City Scenes
Health Claims
Friendship
Plants
Money
Exotic
Numbers
Initials
Slogans
Outrageous Claims
Bargains
Contented Smokers
Highways
Historical Places
Cars

Museum collections

ith all the new museums cropping up, be they public or private, there is no doubt in my mind that a museum dedicated to cigar labels with their broad spectrum of themes and quality of art is long overdue. The Gundlach Group, owners of the spectacular Klingenberg Litho archives in Germany is planning one dedicated to Stone Lithography with a possible site in Bielefeld, Germany, but that is down the road. Until then, or, if you don't want to travel to Germany, there are a number of museums, universities and libraries that own cigar label collections.

As I am sure you are aware, almost 90% of any museum's collections are in the "back room" so you must always inquire of the curators if they have a collection of cigar art. If they do, they will usually give you a private showing with some advance notice on you part. Surprisingly enough, I have never visited a museum that did not have some cigar memorabilia in their collections, from the Chicago Historical Society with Lincoln labels to the Custer Museum in Monroe, Michigan whose hero appeared on a few early cigar labels.

Public libraries should not be overlooked either, since they also accept a variety of donations. In fact, the Cleveland Public Library has an outstanding cigar band collection which I would have never been aware of if it hadn't come up in conversation during one of my research missions. So ask your local museum, historical society public library or university if they have any ephemeral collections containing cigar labels and I'm sure you'll probably be surprised. They might even want to deaccession it to you, or, on the other hand, you could always donate some of your duplicates!

Here are a few institutions that have cigar art in their archives:

1. Smithsonian Institute, Washington, DC
2. Museum of American Folk Art, New York, NY
3. University of South Florida, Tampa, FL
4. Key West Historical Society, Key West, FL
5. Art Gallery of Windsor, Windsor, Ontario, Canada

PUBLICATIONS

In an effort to broaden your library of information concerning these fascinating artworks and their growth in popularity, here is a listing of some publications that had feature stories about cigar label art.

Fortune, March 1933
One of the earliest "awareness" stories recognizing cigar labels as superior artworks. This issue has a full four page spread of actual stone litho prints.
Esquire, February 1949
Two page story in color showing dozens of rare and coveted labels.
Eros, Summer 1962
This hardbound issue is a unique collectible in itself since only four issues were published by Ralph Ginzburg. Includes six full color pages of exotic women on cigar labels.
Collector's News, September 1977
Cover story with colored pictures of rare cigar labels.
Potentials in Marketing, September 1978
Cigar art featured on cover-full color.
American Heritage, December 1978
Cleveland Press, March 16, 1979
Full page story, first page of Connoisseur Section.
Cleveland Plain Dealer, Sunday Magazine, April 1, 1979
Six page story in full color devoted to cigar art.
Wall Street Journal, September 7, 1979
Front page feature story on the dramatic growth of cigar labels on the collectibles market, 3/4 page story plus graphics.
Milwaukee Journal, Sunday Magazine, June 29, 1980
Five page story in full color.
Cincinnati Enquirer, June 27, 1981
Front page story.
Smokeshop News, June 1982
Greensburg (PA) *Tribune Review*, September 26, 1982
Western Reserve, November-December, 1982
Junior Achievement, April 1983
Story and pictures of youth earning thousands of dollars framing and selling cigar art.
Medina County (OH) *Gazette*, January 2, 1985
Two page story.
Elyria (OH) *Chronical Telegram*, Sunday, February 10, 1985
Cover story in full color.
Michiana/South Bend Tribune, June 16, 1985
Five page color story in Sunday Magazine.
The Detroit News, August 24, 1985
Front page story.
Akron (OH) *Beacon Journal*, August 25, 1985
Six page story in full color in Sunday Magazine.
Tiffin (OH) *Advertiser-Tribune*, October 23, 1986
Toldeo (OH) *Blade*, July 19-25, 1987
Four page story in full color in Sunday Magazine.
Time-Life Encyclopedia of Collectibles, Vol. 4

INDEX

Page numbers in italics refer to illustrations.

PICTURE CREDITS

Courtesy of Avi Greenbaum Collection: *Harrison & Reid,* Political label *Cleveland & Stevenson,* Political label; Courtesy of Leonard L. Lasko Collection: *Hey-Yea-Get A Lead,* Hughie Jennings label; Courtesy of Dr. Tony Hyman Collection: Inside Pennsylvania cigar factory, Inside cigar store; Courtesy of Dr. Glen Westfall Collection: Lector-Cigar Factory Reader, Inside Tampa Cigar Factory, Cuesta-Rey Factory; Courtesy of Thomas Vance Collection: *Sanchez & Haya Factory #1* label, *Tampa Life, Monroe Doctrine, El Biscayne, Los Tres, Treaty Bond;* Courtesy of Drs. Bernhard and Bina von Schubert: Klingenberg conference room, Klingenberg logo, Klingenberg sample book, Klingenberg artists, Klingenberg flatbed presses, Klingenberg stock room; Courtesy of John Grossman Collection, copyright of *The Gifted Line: Hans Wagner, Little Nigger, Golf Links, Texie, Lady Speed, Speed King, Black Bat, Car Line, Merry Christmas-Happy New Year, Solid Shot, Rough Riders, Prairie, Mrs. Jack Frost, Charles M. Russell, Aero, Palace Court, Snow Man, First Round, Clown;* Courtesy of Annabelle Stewart: Blaine & Annabelle Stewart in their "Buckeye" Factory, Hicksville, Ohio.

THE AUTHOR

Although he has only been active full-time in the art world for the past ten years as a wholesaler of 75 to 700 year old graphics, Joe Davidson's love of the arts was recognized almost 40 years ago when he won a scholarship to the famous Cleveland Institute of Art. His pursuit of the arts was interrupted by the outbreak of the Korean War, and upon his discharge from the U.S. Navy, he was encouraged to pursue a career in marketing. After 20 years in the Fortune 500 world, having served as both a marketing manager and Director of Education, Joe finally became an entrepreneur and created Aaron's Archives, a rare art distributorship named after his son, who was born in the same year as his new company. Davidson travels the globe constantly searching for new discoveries but also finds time in his busy schedule to serve as Gifted Children's Coordinator for Mensa, the high I.Q. society, and as Executive in Residence at Bowling Green and Kent State Universities in Ohio.